Childhood and
Postcolonization

CHANGING IMAGES OF EARLY CHILDHOOD
Series Editor: Nicola Yelland

Also published in the series:

RETHINKING PARENT AND CHILD
CONFLICT
Susan Grieshaber

CHILDHOOD AND POSTCOLONIZATION:
*Power, Education, and Contemporary
Practice*
Gaile S. Cannella and Radhika Viruru

Childhood and Postcolonization

Power, Education, and Contemporary Practice

Gaile S. Cannella & Radhika Viruru

RoutledgeFalmer

NEW YORK AND LONDON

Published in 2004 by
RoutledgeFalmer
29 West 35th Street
New York, NY 10001
www.routledge-ny.com

Published in Great Britain by
RoutledgeFalmer
11 New Fetter Lane
London EC4P 4EE
www.routledgefalmer.com

Printed in the United States of America on acid-free paper.
Typesetting: Jack Donner, BookType

10 9 8 7 6 5 4 3 2 1

Library of Congress Cataloging-in-Publication Data

Cannella, Gaile Sloan, 1951–
    Childhood and postcolonization : power, education, and contemporary practice / by
Gaile S. Cannella, Radhika Viruru
        p. cm. — (Changing images of early childhood)
Includes bibliographical references and index.
ISBN 0-415-93346-3 (alk paper) — ISBN 0-415-93347-1 (pbk : alk paper)
    1. Early childhood education—Social aspects—United States. 2. Child
development—United States. 3. Postcolonialism—United States. 4. Constructivism
(Education)—United States. I. Viruru, Radhika, 1964- II. Title. III. Series.

LB1139.25.C36 2004
372.21—dc22
                                                                        20041839

CONTENTS

SERIES EDITOR'S INTRODUCTION

Early childhood education has long been organized and justified around the principles of developmentally appropriate practice (DAP), which was founded in the developmental psychology literature from the early part of the past century. The theories of learning and socialization inherent to this literature were conceptualized in vastly different social and economic contexts. Although we are now in the 21st century, education often seems to be caught in a time warp, and justifications for the continued use of outdated practices and attitudes need to be challenged. DAP privileged certain ways of being and knowing that did not recognize the diverse qualities of children and their families in a global context. In doing so it had the effect of alienating the qualities of diversity that should be celebrated, and further suggested that there was a universal state that we should be striving for that was based on Western ways of doing and knowing. In recent times these contentions have been challenged and early childhood education is coming to be known for its openness to new ideas, with the multidisciplinary nature of the field facilitating the process of re-conceptualization. The terrain of early childhood has been remodeled significantly over the past decade, and alternative views and perspectives are beginning to have an impact on practices and pedagogies.

The changing images of early childhood are reflected in the books that will comprise this series, since they challenge and confront educators with a wide range of topics. This series will enable early childhood professionals to engage contemporary ideas and practices from alternative perspectives from those that have been traditionally associated with the education of young children and their families. This series provides opportunities to critique aspects of the field that many early childhood educators have accepted as being beyond question, as well to as act as a catalyst for contemporary interrogations and investigations. The ideas contained in the books will incorporate a wide range of theoretical perspectives that are particularly appropriate to life in the postmodern world. Additionally, issues that have been taboo (e.g., sexuality) or only viewed from one perspective (e.g., moral development) will be presented. In this way the multidisciplinary perspective of the field becomes evident. Today instead of being influenced solely by the psychological perspective, early childhood education benefits from the ideas that have emerged from other disciplines such as anthropology, cultural studies, sociology, and philosophy. This has enriched the capacity of early childhood educators to respond to the new demands of contemporary times with pedagogies and practices that are appropriate to the varying and changing needs and interests of young children and their families. The books in this series will assist students and professionals in the field of early childhood to engage in such dialogues from an informed base. The subjects covered will consider contemporary theoretical perspectives and demonstrate their relevance to everyday practices and in doing so enable us to create learning environments that are underpinned by a respect for all, through equity and social justice.

The goals of the series are clearly exemplified in the current volume, *Childhood and Postcolonization: Power, Education, and Contemporary Practice* by Gaile Cannella and Radhika Viruru. The authors challenge the ways in which we have conceptualized childhood and disempowered children by regarding them as a cohort separate to adults who need to be guided to reproduce the dominant norms we have established in society. This book presents the essence of postcolonial theory and discusses its orgins. The authors present new ways of engaging children that are not controlling or patronizing. This irrevocably leads to a discussion of the ways in which we exert power over children, especially in institutional contexts like schooling that have strong parallels to colonizing powers of past regimes. A fundamental question that arises from this book is What gives some people the right to determine *who* other people are and what they should do? This contemporary view of childhood and children leads us to reconsider and challenge what we have assumed to be the "basic truths" that have controlled much of our behavior, for example, capitalism, consumerism, gender, and educational practices such as the overuse of standardized testing. Cannella and Viruru do not seek to set up new truths but rather ask readers and early childhood educators to engage in a constant critique about our knowledge base and the ways in which it is perpetuated. They provide one alternative way of doing this and present us with new challenges and questions so that we are able to reexamine our practices with the goal of moving forward to a more inclusive conceptualization of childhood.

Nicola Yelland
RMIT University

INTRODUCTION:
Viewing Childhood and Education through Postcolonial Critique

I recently had lunch with my seven-year-old daughter at her school. I took her favorite restaurant lunch, although I had also packed her a lunch at home that morning in case I wasn't able to make it. Sitting in the cafeteria, I was appalled; there were rules and restrictions about everything. Each time the woman in charge wanted to remind them of the rules, the children were asked to raise their hands to be allowed to speak. The rules were that children should use "inside voices" and keep the noise level down, keep their hands and feet to themselves, and always face their own table (turning around was not permitted). There were constant reminders of procedures—students at each table were told when they could buy ice cream, when to stand by the door, when to go to recess. At one point, one of the kindergarten teachers walked through the cafeteria talking to the children. A few minutes later, the children were treated to another reminder of the rules. When the person in charge had finished again reciting the expectations, she asked the children what they were to say to the volunteer who sold ice cream that day. They replied in their loudest voices, "Thank you."

In the midst of all of this controlling activity, there was an announcement that food "seconds" were available in the cafeteria if the children wanted them (seconds being side dishes like grilled cheese sandwiches or rolls). I was surprised that my daughter immediately got up and got in line, for she had plenty of food with her. She stood in line for a long time and came back with one roll, which she hesitantly put in between us. It took me a while to realize that she had brought the bread for me, as I hadn't brought a lunch for myself and she knew that I like rolls. Until I realized what she had done, I thought she was especially hungry (and even that she was being extra picky, as she had two

1

lunches in front of her). I thought then of how often we had talked in our family about how it was considered inhospitable to let a guest leave without having something to eat or drink, after all, I was her guest at school. I know that part of what stood in the way of my seeing her behavior for what it was even though she is my daughter, was because she is seven years old and a child, and we are taught not to expect empathy or mature feelings from children.

—Radhika Viruru

It is because of incidents such as this that we chose to write this book. As early childhood educators, drawn to this field because of its insistence on putting children first, we have become increasingly concerned about the consequences of labeling younger human beings as "children." What kinds of limitations and lost possibilities take place when this labeling occurs? In the epigraph the status of child is used to signify and legitimate the regulation of the behavior of particular human beings. Further, the label and all that is associated with it limits one's expectations of what those who have been labeled can do. We are trained to think that children are egocentric, easily distractible, noisy, and curious and that our job is to be accepting of these characteristics while moving children forward. Our hope is that this book will raise questions regarding the way we have limited and even physically colonized those who are younger. What is controlled, lost, disqualified, and even erased through our expectations? How do our beliefs about childhood serve as violence against children, a kind of epistemic violence that limits human possibilities, freedom, and actions?

WHO ARE WE AND WHAT ARE OUR PERSPECTIVES?

The field of early childhood education (and the knowledge bases associated with it, like developmental psychology) has been a professional home to us for many years. Through the 15 years we have known each other, we have found that we share a reason for choosing the field of education, and specifically early childhood education—the continued attempts by people in the field to put the child first, to recognize that those who are younger are human beings who have not always been heard, cared for, or even acknowledged. For many years I (Gaile Cannella) was a strong proponent of what would now be considered "developmentally appropriate practice." The first graduate class that Radhika Viruru took was on constructivist methods in early childhood education. Despite also coming from very different backgrounds (White/of color, so-called first/third world), both of us experienced a growing dissatisfaction with the knowledge base from which we were working, as it seemed too limited and too isolating, too simple and too monocultural. This dissatisfaction led us in many different directions, all marked, however, with a respect for complexity and difference related to human beings and their world.

We are aware that many of our readers will, at least at first, judge post-colonialism and related perspectives as irrelevant to the understanding of childhood. Our aims, however, have been and continue to be to do the kind of work and engage in the kind of scholarship that creates more possibilities and avenues for children; this is the purpose of our post-colonial critique. We believe that we must stop looking at childhood as an isolated phenomenon, intelligible only through the lenses of "experts" who have studied the child through the dominant telescope of Western discourses like psychology. We believe that we must start thinking about those who are younger as people who are part of a much larger and complex whole, as linked to and influencing the larger and more complex world. Otherwise, we are not doing justice to the lives of children and to their existence as human beings. As scholars, we are aware that we all have ideological "agendas" and biases. We also believe that an awareness of these biases and continued critical attempts to analyze and honestly face them are necessary as we would share our agendas but would avoid the imposition of one "truth-oriented" perspective. It does not always follow that the paths and avenues that we chose to explore would be the ones that others would choose. However, we hope that being open about the reasons for our approach will render this subject more intelligible. We also hope that the reader does not take our perspectives, approaches, or the information that we share as an attempt to generate a new truth; it is our desire to provide thoughts and possibilities that are open to critique, that would generate new ideas and previously unthought-of possibilities, and that will most likely be different for each reader.

We made a conscious decision to begin this book by stepping outside the world of childhood theories as we have predominantly known them to look for different possibilities. Once we started to look further afield, we actually found that from an interdisciplinary perspective crossing boundaries does not lead far from where we started (with our concern for those who are younger). We found that children were certainly an invisible presence in the discourses and actions surrounding colonialism/imperialism or country development, as well as contemporary expert intellectual, accountability, and economic rhetoric. Many extreme impositions of power (i.e., taking over other countries and reorganizing their ways of existing) have been legitimated in the name of children—to ensure a better future for them, to save their souls, to teach their parents how to live their lives. Similar kinds of rhetoric remain without even the necessity of a physical imposition of power (perhaps with capitalists and moralists impositions), as governments justify their decisions in terms of ensuring that the world is a safer place or that individuals be made accountable for systemic societal structures (therefore denying equities or change).

Furthermore, we have found that for many years the lives of children were impacted by the figure of "Empire"; for example, males were raised to be healthy and strong so that they could go out and subdue foreign infidels and bring glory to "crown and country." The colonization of most parts of the non-Western world (and lands that came to dominate the West like the United States) and the emergence of the most commonly accepted discourses about children took place in the same historical period and served similar purposes. We believe that it is, at least, somewhat naive to think that colonialist practices and beliefs about the "child," coming as they did from the same source, had little to do with each other. Thus, we propose that the simplistic, ahistorical/apolitical acceptance and perpetuation of the "child" as construct symbolizes the acceptance of the dominate imperialist ways of viewing and interpreting the world. We were struck over and again by how little respect for human life and dignity was accorded in the truths that had impacted so much of the world. The powers that showed so little compunction in dividing and carving up the world could hardly be expected to show extraordinary sensitivity and wisdom in the ways in which they organized human life (specifically the study and interpretation of it). In the same way that geographical realities were created to serve the interests of imperial capitalist powers, we believe that "human" realities (childhood being one of them) have been fashioned in a similar manner.

We are aware that this is a giant leap for many of our colleagues. Educators (and often developmental psychologists) are probably the least likely of all people to want to dominate and colonize anyone, and certainly do not perceive or intend the work they do to be limiting. We share that common commitment with our colleagues, to engage in the kind of work that creates more opportunities for children. What was helpful to us was the recognition that the knowledge base from which we had generally functioned (e.g., developmental theory, educational learning theories) was incomplete and partial, and it invited exploration. Even the most ardent believer of Piaget's theory, for example, never said that it provided us with all of the answers; actually, interpreted in particular ways, the notions of reciprocity, learning through social interaction, and knowledge construction do open the door to cultural knowledge construction (even if not intended). Additionally, the diversity of the population that has been labeled as children seemed to ensure that the search for knowledge would always be respected.

We know that to many it is offensive and insulting to suggest that the work that one has spent a lifetime (in many cases) doing, with great honesty and sincerity, can be called colonizing. It is partly for this reason that we chose to focus the first section of this book on what might be called the "larger picture." We hope that these global, integrated discussions will give readers a sense of the magnitude of the imperialist enterprises from within which all of us function. Most of the global population has and continues to be influenced by processes of colonization/imperialism and postcolonization. We believe very strongly that these histories, practices, and contemporary conditions must first be understood to fully comprehend their impact on younger human beings. We must first begin to consider the complex notion of colonialism and Empire to create a disposition that can consider childhood as an imperial construct.

Using breastfeeding as an example, scholars have shown how women in multiple contexts practiced what the West might call extended breastfeeding for many reasons, contraception being one of them. With the intrusion of colonial powers into their realm, the practice was labeled unsanitary, among other things, and discontinued. The consequence has been the birth of more children, condemned as a result of "undereducation" which then depletes the world's resources—condemnations that continue today. Yet, currently in much of the West, breastfeeding is touted as the "best" way to feed babies, while at the same time multinational corporations are extensively marketing baby formula in so-called third world contexts at exorbitant prices. Without awareness of the complexity of this history and the impositions of power related to it, judgments about breastfeeding and the construction of "infant" as concept, as well as the behavior of mothers, are oversimplified as scientific truth that is revealed (and controlled) by the West. This is just one example, but we believe that many of the issues that surround the study and construction of childhood are similarly complex.

HOW WOULD WE EXPLAIN THIS BOOK?

The very act of writing this book is fraught with colonialist/imperialist problems like those just mentioned. In the same sense that we have questioned the acceptance of the concept of childhood as an imperialist way of functioning, the writing of books can be critiqued. As we explore in a later chapter, the very concept of literacy has unmistakable colonial connotations. Although we have accepted the form of the book, we also hope that the book's contents challenge some of the assumptions about what books are and what they should do.

First and foremost, we did not write the book to set up postcolonial ways of studying childhood as a new kind of truth or a place where all the answers could be found and problems solved. Our attraction to postcolonial theory was precisely its repudiation of such truth-oriented points of view and its willingness to acknowledge the uncertainties and complexities that necessarily accompany any study of human behavior. Nor do we think that simply broadening current views of childhood to include examples and studies from hitherto unstudied contexts and unthought disciplinary relationships is some type of answer. That perspective would be using postcolonial theory to construct the third world as a new object of investigation, a trap that Spivak (1996) cautions against. Our construction of connections between childhood and postcolonialism is of a different nature. We ask the reader to engage in a constant critique of our knowledge and our ways of discovering knowledge. We also call for a continuous reexamination of the biases that cause us to privilege one set of knowledge over the other.

This book is also an attempt to bring into focus the unchallenged legacies of colonialism, mostly the fixing of socially constructed categories as truth. In the first section, we look at what are considered some of the basic truths that govern much of human behavior—the concepts of gender and time, the very definition of what it means to be a human being, and the roots and the legacies of those ideas. Some of these ideas have become so much a part of the fabric of everyday existence that questioning them seems ridiculous. But, we believe, it is only through a commitment to serious reexamination that we can move toward a thoughtful and more inclusive study of childhood. Perhaps some may question why we did not include childhood as one of those truths to be reexamined early on in the book. There are multiple reasons. For one, we believe that most people reading this book are already concerned about childhood, and as such cannot help but think about the implications for childhood within the framework that we follow. In later chapters, after we have had an opportunity to thoroughly consider the complexities of colonialist and imperialist practice, we do more detailed examination of issues relating to children. However, we continually remind you that prescriptiveness would be not only contradictory to the theoretical positions we are trying to explain, but also insulting to the possibilities that human beings can generate. We believe that it is both more effective and more respectful to suggest possibilities to readers than to lay out direct actions (in addition to being more consistent with postcolonial critique).

A major theme throughout this book is the question of power. We believe that fundamental to the study of childhood is the question: What gives some people the right to determine *who* other people are (determinations like the fundamental nature of childhood) and to decide what is right for others? The answer to this question may seem obvious, but it is usually hidden within both physical and intellectual domination, especially as related to those who are younger. If one believes that there are fundamental truths about human beings that exist and that rigorous study is the way to reveal those truths, then the Western scientific study of childhood that has taken place and that forms the basis for many of our current understandings of childhood makes some sense. If, instead, one focuses on power (e.g., colonialist, imperialist, capitalist, psychological, adult, and otherwise) and what to do in situations when one group has more power than another, entirely different questions and knowledges are enacted. For example, why have we (in fields concerned with younger human beings) not focused more on ways in which to make children's perspectives a much larger part of the discourse on childhood? Or, rather than exhaustive studies on whether children can tell if a tall, thin glass has more liquid than a short, fat one, why haven't questions like possibilities for lowering the voting age been looked at in more detail? Postcolonial theory serves as a very useful resource for those interested in questions of power and how its influence on the most shaky of ethical grounds often goes unquestioned. In later chapters, we look at what happens when subalterns speak and the ways in which power has been exercised to silence them. We would ask what this silencing means for those who are younger. Attempts to disrupt dominant discourses about childhood have already been handled in a similar fashion. Critiques of developmentally appropriate practice are currently ignored, whenever possible, by many in the field. Currently, standardized testing is a further excellent example (see discussion within this book). However, as colonial histories have demonstrated, informed resistance can be successful—hegemonic power can be challenged and changes made.

Depending upon the perspective of the reader, there may seem to be holes in the content of the book—connections that have not been explicitly made, explanations that have not been offered, or obvious ties that have not been named. We believe that by not drawing conclusions, we open the door to multiple conclusions, not just our own necessarily limited ones. We have also learned a great deal (through the process of writing this book and other experiences) about the power of silence. Many of the ideas that we wish to invoke, we believe, are best accomplished when not spoken directly. The very idea that language is the only form of communication through which people can express important ideas is one of those foundations of imperialism that we wish to challenge. Furthermore, we believe that children have often been judged as "incomplete" due to their lack of language skills. What we are trying to attempt through a book like this is a glimpse of the possibilities that the unspoken might offer, that the previously unthought might generate.

Thus, in the first section of the book we lay out a theoretical framework about postcolonial theory and its implications for our ways of viewing the world (while at the same time even invoking the limitations constructed in the Western notion of theory). Our aims are to provide theoretical information that would familiarize our readers with postcolonial theory in general, but also with some of its lesser-known aspects, such as how processes of colonization have impacted the academic disciplines we take for granted (the disciplines that have grounded our construction of both "child" and "education"). In Chapter 3 we look specifically at issues of power, with an extensive consideration of Foucault's work, supplemented with a consideration of studies of power in colonial contexts. In the concluding sections of the chapter, we look at what has happened when subalterns have tried to speak. Again, we would emphasize that the aim of this book is not only to inform readers about how imperialism has impacted the world in which we live but also to provoke debate about how this is directly or indirectly related to children. We provide more specific discussion of the connections between colonialism/imperialism and childhood/education in Part II of the book, and in Part III we offer possibilities for action in classrooms with children, for the reconceptualization and reconstruction of teacher education, and finally for the reconceptualization of the ways in which we do research with children.

Decolonialization is difficult. Even the naming of specific actions can prove contradictory and result in the reconstitution of colonialist practice. We challenge the reader to create unthought-of and unnamed possibilities with and for younger human beings, as well as for all of us. The work is important, even vital, but there are no direct steps that everyone can follow—no easy actions that fall under "what works," no manual for appropriateness. We can simply (yet, complexly and even ambiguously) learn, think, challenge, contest, and join together to explore possibilities, to challenge oppressive power, and to rethink who we are and what is important to us both personally and professionally.

Part I
Defining Postcolonialism and Cultural Critique

1
COLONIALISM/POSTCOLONIALISM:
Historical and Contemporary Conditions

When the Portuguese set foot in Brazil, there were five million indigenous people. . . . Today they number 330,000.

—as cited in Young, 2001, p. 1 (from *Survival* (May 2000)

Colonialism is a concept that many of us in the United States either associate patriotically with the settling of America, or associate with past conquests that no longer occur. We would even propose that many groups of people around the world whose lives have been privileged through economic, social, and political circumstances would deny and even be unaware that colonialist impositions are contemporary issues. Certainly, individuals, families, and communities struggling to survive, work, and be educated barely have time to consider notions of colonialism or Empire. How could colonialism be related to contemporary life, either locally or globally? For adults or children? Yet, physical colonialism is so extensive that the impact can be felt all around the world. Imperialism continues to be played out in economic structures, societal institutions, and ways that people view themselves, as well as through continued physical occupation in various locations of the world. Further, imperialist thought invades the daily lives of individuals and groups all over the globe.

In this chapter, we begin by explaining the history of physical colonization and the continued impact of this imperialist practice on the lives of real people living today even after most physical colonialism has ended. The terminologies and perspectives associated with postcolonialism are explained with an in-depth discussion of postcolonial critique.

THE EXTENT AND IMPACT OF PHYSICAL COLONIZATION

We begin by critiquing the notion that we could provide an accurate history of colonialism. Is there one version or perspective on colonialist/imperialist events? Are there simple or even complex truths about the extent and impact of colonialism? These questions represent the way we have learned to use postcolonial critique to challenge truth-oriented disciplines, including history. (The will to power embedded in the construction of academic disciplines is discussed in Chapter 2.) Although critique of dominant disciplines is necessary, we will use the traditional notion of history, which would attempt to closely approximate physical events. Recognizing that this orientation toward truth can be colonizing, we believe that providing some feeling for the massive physical influence of colonialist practice can also lead to broader constructions of history, continued critique, and the construction of decolonial practices.

Imperialist powers either controlled or occupied 90% of the world at the beginning of World War I. This occupation was violently imposed over a 500-year period and has a history of slavery, unimaginable and unnamed deaths, oppression, and forced migration (Young, 2001). Racism was institutionalized and cultural genocide legitimated as Enlightenment belief in patriarchal superiority reigned (Cannella, 1997; Chaliand and Rageau, 1995; Ferro, 1997). European intellect, culture, and understanding of the world were considered more advanced—superior to others. According to Mohanram (1999), by 1800 55% of the earth's land surface had been claimed by the imperial powers of western and southern Europe. Further, in the 19th century, Europe acquired new territories at the rate of 210,000 square kilometers a year. Magdoff (1978) estimates that 55 million Europeans moved to different parts of the globe between 1820 and 1920.

Young (2001) suggests that it is not a coincidence that European imperial powers turned upon themselves, attempting to conquer one another only when there was essentially no place left on the globe to conquer. "Fascism was a form of colonialism that was brought home to Europe" (Young, 2001, p. 2), as Germany attempted to create Empire during World War II (Cesaire, 1972). Although Italy and Japan basically lost their prewar possessions and the remaining colonial powers (e.g., Britain, France, the Netherlands, Belgium, Denmark) decolonized following

World War II, many countries remained closely tied to their former colonizers. For example, although India's independence in 1947 from Britain began the process of decolonization that is for the most part over, there are many legacies, both visible and intangible, territorial and human, that remain. The United States is a very complex and unique example, being both a former colony, whose indigenous peoples were all but eliminated, as well as a contemporary colonizing power (e.g., control over Puerto Rico).

Even though physical decolonization seemed to happen quickly (colonizers moved out and appeared to no longer attempt physical occupation), the list of locations remaining under a dependent colonial status is long. Subordinate status is signified in a variety of ways through labels like dependent or unincorporated territory, overseas department, or trust. Examples of these include British Gibralter, Dutch Antilles, French Guiana, and U.S. Virgin Islands (Young, 2001). Further, in the contemporary world, less obvious, more hidden (although no less dangerous) conditions exist. These struggles are of various types and origins but include problems caused by conditions that were either created or compounded by imperial powers, such as the struggles between groups who were historically colonized. Examples include the focus by the Catholic minority in Northern Ireland to become part of a united Ireland, struggles for equal rights by various groups of Aboriginal peoples, and the conflict between Palestine and Israel.

Finally, colonization transformed and impoverished the structure of economies, generated privileged knowledges and discourses, and established imperialist institutions. Peoples, cultures, and countries changed. When physical decolonization occurred, there was no possibility of achieving some form of precolonial state of being (either metaphorically or physically). The remnants of Empire were embedded within contemporary societies all around the globe.

THE ILLUSION OF UNDERSTANDING: RELUCTANTLY DEFINING TERMS

Unfortunately, we cannot proceed without defining or at least specifying our referents in using certain terms. The idea of definition invokes precisely the kind of images that are challenged by postcolonial critique—an enlightenment/modernist dualism (accurately defining or not), a colonialist scientific heritage (grounded in Western male, linear truth orientations toward the world), and a way of organizing thought that is alien to many people around the globe. However, many of us have learned to expect this way of functioning. We know that most of our readers will ask What is meant by colonialism? Imperialism? What is postcolonialism? What do they mean by decolonizing? A full discussion of the many constructs that are relevant to postcolonial critique is beyond the scope of the book (see the work of Young, 2001); however, a summary of constructs, issues, and ideas is necessary. We begin by providing our overall impressions of the related "-isms" (colonialism, imperialism, neocolonialism), however Western that might appear. We then address constructs that are often used throughout postcolonial discourse.

Colonialism and Imperialism

Although both colonialism and imperialism involve the takeover, subjugation, and control of one group of people by another, at least simplistically the purpose for control can be differentiated between the two practices. The physical occupation of India by the British and the conquest of South America by Spain and Portugal were attempts to civilize and exploit, to establish Empire, and as such, created imperialist structures. In contrast are such projects as the British settlements in North America and Australia that were undertaken for multiple reasons (e.g., fleeing the established church, as a location for convicts), but lacked any kind of ideological mission that would bring civilization to the natives or channel new financial resources to the center of the Empire. Thus, colonies established for the purpose of settlement can be characterized as colonial projects, and those established for the purpose of exploitation as imperial projects. If one adopts this simplistic framework of thinking, then much of postcolonial theory and writing would be more accurately labeled postimperial (Young, 2001).

However, colonialism was not a benign practice. For example, although the pilgrims settled North America with the purpose of establishing their own rule away from the Empire, indigenous peoples were exterminated. Although the actions may not have been created to support the Empire, certainly the results could be called an imperialist imposition. Similarly, in so-called settler colonies like Rhodesia and South Africa, the process of settlement by the new arrivals caused mass dissettlement for the original inhabitants. Colonialism, even if conceived as distinct from imperialism, still involves fundamental acts of geographical violence on human beings (Said, 1993).

Loomba (1998) also cautions against drawing simplistic distinctions between colonialism and imperialism since both practices are too complex to pin down. Although economic and power motives were no doubt primary in countries reaching out and expanding to different parts of the globe, there were also internal social issues that drove this effort. In Britain, for example, the question of population was a major factor influencing outward expansion. Colonies were places where surplus populations (often those labeled undesirable) could be safely exported. Thus, the colonization of the world was also tied to the need for colonial powers to export their internal social conflicts. Further, colonization and imperialism, although widely conceived as originating in Europe, are not purely European. Spanish imperialism in Latin America was influenced by the Islamic Jihad that led to the Moorish colonization of Spain. Colonialism and the construction of Empire have been recurring features in human history, albeit in different forms. The Roman Empire, the Aztec Empire, and rule by a royal family in Imperial Russia are illustrations.

Imperialism has multiple meanings and multiple histories, but is most often "characterized by an exercise of power, either through direct conquest or (latterly) through political and economic influence that effectively amounts to a similar form of domination" (Young, 2001, p. 27). French imperialism was both progressive and dismissive. French actions rested on the premise that all human beings were equal and shared a common humanity; conversely, the definition of humanity was based on individualist notions of enlightenment freedom that tended to disqualify the variety of ways human beings lived their lives (especially in the colonies). The French spoke a language of equality yet imposed their own views of humanity on others without hesitation. Additionally, British imperialism can be interpreted as inscribing a racist ideology because the determiner of what was considered to be civilized or not was skin color. This justified the imposition of continued colonialism because the difference (one's skin color) would never be overcome. This perspective was justified as a liberal form of imperialism, in that occupied native cultures were "respected" by being left alone to practice their own culture (with the exception of religion and, of course, economics!).

Another distinguishing feature of imperialism, and possibly the major reason for the existence of postcolonial theory, is that the establishment of colonies for the purpose of exploitation did much more than simply extract wealth (Loomba, 1998). Economies were restructured setting up a flow of both humans and capital that produced economic imbalances that made the industrial growth of Europe possible. Such systems resulted in conditions in which direct internal political control by the colonizers was not necessary because economic control was more secure and lasting. Further, this created a global system of capitalist imperialism through which capitalist economies established colonies that could provide human resources (like labor) to maintain the colonizers capital growth (Lenin, 1965 [1917]).

Smith (1999) also comments on the relationship between imperialism and colonialism, viewing colonialism as but one expression of imperialism. As an economic endeavor, imperialism is described as securing markets for European products. Correspondingly, colonialism was the system for establishing control over the populations who would be the market, the "outpost" for imperialism (p. 23). This perspective combines colonialism and imperialism to create methods that would legitimate the subjugation of large populations of people, a subjugation that was reinforced through the categorizing of native populations (the legislation of identities as indigenous or not). The economic power interest of the colonizer is the driving force. Further, imperialism can be located "within the enlightenment spirit" (p. 23) that assumed scientific progress and reasoned intellectual superiority. Large numbers of people were judged as lacking, deficient, not advanced—both at home and in the colonies. The enterprise did not just establish domination over native populations but also ensured that Europeans were kept under control—kept in the service of Empire.

Finally, Loomba (1998) explains another way of distinguishing between and connecting colonialism and imperialism, suggesting that the two practices ought to be separated in spatial terms. In her distinction, imperialism is considered to be the phenomenon that takes place in the metropolis that at least partially caused the colonizer to seek "others" to dominate and control. Thus, countries that undertook projects of outward expansion were considered imperialist. The result of imperialism is colonialism; the places, spaces, bodies, and minds that have been affected by imperialism are colonial. This connection is especially useful because a major theme of postcolonial critique can then be understood—the notion that imperialism can function without colonies, a perspective that is embedded thoughout our postcolonial analysis of the construction of child.

Neocolonialism

The European imperial powers could no longer afford (e.g., financially or politically because the United States wanted economic expansion) to continue direct domination of other countries following World War II. A neocolonialism, however, emerged that was, although more subtle, a version of continued Empire. As notions of country development were constructed to assist colonized peoples in movements toward independence, Eurocentric assumptions regarding people, country, culture, progress, and economy dominated. Understandings, forms of assistance, and constructions of appropriate actions were decidedly European and American.

Even more important, the international system of capitalist power (a contemporary Empire) that had been established through imperialism was not challenged (Young, 2001). Although the colonized had provided and continue to have resources, the control of the markets (and ways of viewing the world) were/are centered in places like London and New York. Formerly colonized territories have regained some physical and political independence, but they have remained dependent on major world powers economically. Using Gramsci's (1971; Anderson, 1976–77) definition of political and civil societies, the neocolonial situation simply shifted the power from control by military force (political society) to a condition in which control is maintained by a particular cultural, ideological, and economic elite who are complicit with the international capitalist system (civil society). Control is now maintained through "access to capital and technology" (Young, 2001, p. 47) using organizations like the World Bank, the International Monetary Fund, and the World Trade Organization. As Spivak (1999) explains, neocolonialism is "the largely economic rather than the largely territorial enterprise of imperialism" (p. 3), the latest and perhaps the last stage of Empire.

In 1965, the Ghanaian leader Kwame Nkrumah theoretically examined neocolonialism in his book *Neocolonialism: The Last State of Imperialism.* Just 4 years after Ghana had gained independence (in 1961), Nkrumah attempted to describe the flow of economic power in much of the postcolonial condition. Independence provided the illusion of international sovereignty, yet the economic system remained dependent on international capitalism inscribed during imperialist occupation. Nkrumah further explained that even political policy was directed from outside the country to meet the economic needs of the West. He proposed that the postcolonial era would be characterized by an international division of labor that would be used to maintain the relatively high living standards of the working class in the West. Nkrumah argued that because of American economic power, the contemporary period could be considered American colonialism, Empire without physical colonization. Finally, although Nkrumah described neocolonialism as continued colonial rule using different means, he also proposed that it is the "last hideous gasp" (p. 253) of imperialism. The use of capital for continued exploitation would not simply be detrimental to those who were formerly colonized, but would also eventually drown those doing the exploitation (Nkrumah, 1965; Young, 2001).

In the years since Nkrumah began the discussion of neocolonialism, a succession of economic theories have emerged that have both perpetuated and attempted to explain the power relations between so-called third world countries and their colonizers. Examples include development theory that assumes the importance of modernization, Latin

American and Marxist economic dependency theories that label colonialist power practices as purposeful underdevelopment that would maintain dependency, and world system theory that has attempted to mask exploitation by invoking the greater needs of the world market. Eurocentric, capitalist understandings of the world have been assumed to be correct. Imperialist powers have imposed economic restrictions on postcolonial nations that were not required of the colonizer. For example, the United States functions as if its markets work as ideal democratic entities—without the recognition that the markets have been built on the backs of slaves, women, poor people around the world, and immigrant laborers. In the name of the global market, colonialist powers have been and continue to be reinscribed.

However, social movements like anticolonialism and feminism have helped to generate critical activist and culturalist orientations that go beyond neocolonialism. Multiple ways of interpreting the world have been constructed that challenge Enlightenment logic, linear progress toward advanced development, and assumed superiority. Neocolonialist perspectives remain useful in that they continue to focus on economics and provide a framework for including the cultural and political within economic power analyses (Ngugi, 1981, 1993). Yet, postcolonial critique challenges the boundaries of economics, politics, and culture to combine the social sciences and the humanities, creating a mixture of activist, hybrid discourses that are embedded in action. Discussions of neocolonialism begin the conversation, but postcolonial critique generates possibilities (Arndt, 1987; Young, 2001).

POSTCOLONIALISM AND POSTCOLONIAL CRITIQUE

The term postcolonialism has been contested, legitimated, argued about, and discussed from a variety of perspectives. There are those who believe that the use of the prefix post is not appropriate because physical imperialism still exists, and certainly economic and Western intellectual imperialism permeates the globe. There are others who believe that the postcolonial discussion and construction of theory is very much a Western intellectual endeavor. We certainly agree with both of these points and a variety of others that demonstrate the complexity of the idea. (For additional information see (Appiah, 1992; Loomba, 1998; Shohat, 1992; Sleman, 1994.) However, we believe that the construct as terminology, theoretical disposition, and field of study is important for the recognition of the context in which we all live. Postcolonialism embodies the recognition of the Western imperialist project, followed by historical attempts to physically decolonize, while at the same time leaving nations and peoples living under one form of imperialist political and economic domination that is spreading to include power over identity(ies) and intellect, contemporarily infused with active critique and innovative interventions that would challenge oppression, objectification, and othering (Young, 2001).

Because of its origin on the three southern continents—Africa, Asia, and Latin America—postcolonialism could accurately be called tricontinentalism. Whether labeled postcolonial or tricontinental critique, an action emerges with the purpose of addressing the legacy of colonialism imposed by Western attempts to create Empire over the past 500 years. This particular "will to power" was profound because of the global influence, totalization of diverse societies into one universal, and the imposition of a narrow economic path on societies that previously interpreted human experience, as well as economics, from a range of diverse perspectives. Although some consider colonization to have ended or believe that Western imperialism was just one form of oppression like many others, postcolonial critique recognizes the extraordinary continuing influence of Western imperialism.

> The entire world now operates within the economic system primarily developed and controlled by the west, and it is the continued dominance of the west, in terms of political, economic, military and cultural power, that gives this history a continuing significance. Political liberation did not bring economic liberation—and without economic liberation, there can be no political liberation. (Young, 2001, p. 5)

Committed to developing "new forms of engaged theoretical work" (Young, 2001, p. 11) in the pursuit of social transformation for liberation, the goals are to: contest forms of domination, create equal access, and generate political and cultural identities collectively. Often associated with Marxism, postcolonial theory introduces international rights and focuses on possibilities for a popular socialism rather than the more common coercive forms imposed thus far. The assumption is that political intervention is possible when connections are made across disciplines, between different intellectual traditions, and when activism is employed.

Postcolonial critique is always cognizant of the continued presence of Western expansion and uses comprehensive research into the continued effects of colonization on both colonized and colonizing societies. Politics of the past and present are connected through methods like "archeological retrieval" and "revaluation" (Young, 2001, p. 6). In the

1960s, activists on three continents, black civil rights workers, and feminists adopted the goals and assumptions as they worked for equity and freedom.

Related Constructions

The language used for postcolonial critique both originates across a variety of disciplines and from a range of locations and may be reconceptualized and renamed to provide understandings from marginalized positions. We understand that because of this complexity of usage, postcolonial discourses can be very confusing. Additionally, our attempt to overview postcolonial theory and at the same time use the perspective to critique childhood can be even more confounding. For these reasons, the following are brief discussions of influential constructs that are used to some extent throughout the text. As mentioned at the beginning of this section, postcolonial critique would most often avoid truth-oriented definitions and would even challenge concepts like theory, reason, and logic. The discussions should be taken, therefore, as sites from which to more thoroughly understand our perspectives and discourses rather than as facts that define some type of logical truth. Finally, the list is not complete; we would expect the reader to note constructs that are used throughout and to generate her or his own issues that may require further explanation and study.

Colonialism and Patriarchy. Locating the existence of patriarchy as before the emergence of Western thought, Lerner (1986, 1993) describes the basic assumptions underlying this hierarchical view of the world. Males and females are considered essentially different from each other, with males being stronger, more rational, and naturally superior. Males are considered to be designed for political citizenship and to be those who are qualified to order and control the universe. Aristotle expressed such a belief: "the one rules and the other is ruled; this principle, of necessity extends to all mankind" (1941, p. 1132). When the founding fathers in the United States constructed the Declaration of Independence, rights and liberty were not even considered for women. John Adams illustrated this way of thinking in a discussion with his wife in which he referred to women as another tribe like children, Indians, and Negroes. He even proposed that disorder would result if "masculine systems" were changed (as cited in Butterfield, Friedlaender, & Kline, 1975, p. 123). This same imperialist assumption of superiority has been evidenced in a large number of countries and cultures. Women have been either used for service (in a variety of ways), ignored, or defined "out" throughout the history of the development of Western thought.

The assumptions underlying patriarchy and the construction of women are consistent with the imperialist legitimation of colonialism, if not identical to it. In *Outlaw Culture*, hooks (1994) even stresses the point: "For contemporary critics to condemn the imperialism of the white colonizer without critiquing patriarchy is a tactic that seeks to minimize the particular ways gender determines the specific forms oppression may take" (p. 203).

As feminists, our bias is that Western thought is grounded in patriarchy. The logic of Enlightenment/modernism that has been forced on the colonized is a linear, male-constructed form of reason and hierarchical power that reinforces the notion that one group is superior to another. The list of illustrations is endless (e.g., inequitable pay, control of women's bodies through marriage and reproductive regulation, competitive systems and actions that lead to winners and losers, linear and objective legitimations of science that disqualify subjectivity). While we may not always be referring to patriarchy in our discussions, we believe that the assumptions of patriarchal discourse and practice are prevalent throughout colonialism and imperialism.

Distinctions between the West and the East. The use of West and East as terms of discourse in relation to peoples, locations, and even ways of thinking has been defined and perpetuated by those who have identified with the west (predominately Europeans and Americans). Edward Said's (1978) work examines this distinction as he discusses the construction of the East as the orient and the West as the occident. During colonialism, the orient, meaning the Middle East, was mostly viewed by the British and French as exotic, mysterious, and strange. As with physical colonization, the discourse represents Europe as the center. Enlightenment thought, which espoused particular ideological, scientific, and social positions (see Chapter 4), reinforced this separation between Europeans and their descendants and the rest of the world (those who were not of European descent). The orient/East was represented (and often continues to be) in European art, literature, and thought as exotic, inferior, and the contrast to Europe. In the United States, the distinction between the West and the East was accepted but was more likely to be applied to the Far East. This dichotomous perspective represents the East as the "other," as those who are not as intelligent, powerful, or advanced as those in the West.

Occidentalism, or the discourses of the West, are at the root of the three most common myths currently prevalent: (1) the belief in universal and objective knowledge that can be known; (2) the notion that decolonization has taken place because imperialist powers no longer occupy; and (3) the belief that parts of the world are still underdeveloped. Beginning with Spanish and Portuguese expeditions in the 1400s, a global process of defining the political agenda of what can be called "Western thought" emerged and came to dominate the world as we know it today. As part of this process, both internal and external borders were constructed and reconstructed, internally against such populations as Jews, Arabs, and Gypsies, and externally separating the north from the south in Europe (labeling Latin cultures as "less than" northern cultures). An essential part of this distinction is the process of nation-building. Within the confines of the so-called West, the emphasis was on defining the rights of citizens and setting up systems of parliamentary democracies. On the other side of the world, however, the process of nation building (imposed by the West) consisted more of enforcing imperial rule and subjecting citizens to authoritarian rules within their own countries, all supposedly in the name of establishing the foundation for their own development.

While we do not agree with a colonialist dualism (whether imposed by the West or accepted by the East), we use the term West throughout the book when dominant ways of thinking, being, or interpreting the world that have been generated and imposed by the West are being discussed. Often (but not always) these views are also linear and stereotypically male oriented. The West has generated a variety of ways of viewing the world, and we do not want to imply that these views are good or bad. However, we do believe (1) that Western understandings (as with all perspectives) include both possibilities and limitations, and (2) that beliefs from any understanding of the world should not be imposed on everyone as if the best, most moral, or most advanced.

Capitalism. Although by no means endorsing the idea of universal truths, postcolonial scholars have stressed that capitalism has become in many ways the one great undecapable power (at least for our times). Spivak (1999) goes so far as to comment that "there is no state on the globe today that is not part of the capitalist economic system" (p. 85). The word capitalism evokes multiple meanings, expecially given the number of localities in which meanings are defined. In a variety of ways, this definitional difficulty creates circumstances in which living outside the boundaries of capitalism is most likely impossible. However, within postcolonial scholarship there are some common understandings useful in trying to grapple with the effects of the unescapable power. Grosfoguel and Cervantes-Rodriguez (2002) locate the foundation of what they call the "capitalist world system" in the Spanish/Portuguese expansion to the Americas in the 16th century, a time frame that also included the expulsion of those identified as Arabic and Jewish from Spain in the name of "blood purity" and the creation of the racialized categories of "White, Negro and Indian" (p. xii). According to these authors, the creation of international divisions of labor that perpetuate this capitalist world system and the creation of globalized racialized identities are intertwined and continue to dominate the world. On the one hand, the newly formed nations in the Americas and the Western world developed and refined such concepts as citizenship and democracy. Simultaneously, however, communities and cultures of color were subjected to continuous foreign invasions/colonization and labor exploitation, all in the name of progress and development (even legitimated as necessary for that advancement).

According to Marx, the prerequisites of democracy and freedom were necessary foundations for capitalism to take root. Capitalism is seen as an inevitably global process that gradually spreads around the world. Whenever difference is encountered, it is neutralized and canceled, or more dangerously, converted into "sets of preference" (Chakrabarty, 2000, p. 49). According to Chakrabarty, Marx's understanding of capitalism was rooted in the Enlightenment and consequent concepts of "juridical equality and the abstract political rights of citizenship" (p. 50). People in the capitalist world have to be politically "free" to choose to engage in the labor that capitalism creates. This freely chosen labor works in the interests of captialism by perpetuating it as the common dominator extracted from human beings across cultures. This concept of abstract labor, regulated by well-defined processes, changes the ways of societies. A disciplinary power (see Chapter 5) is created through "codes of factory regulation, the relationship between machinery and men, stage legislation guiding the organization of factory lives' (p. 55). This capitalist labor is regulated by principles of efficiency and organization, creating the belief that human activity is measurable, homogenous, and marketable. Postcolonial scholars believe that this categorization is extremely dangerous. As an example, capitalist production perspectives create biological categories like women, children, and adult males that define and regulate human beings based on productive capacity and market value (however arbitrarily chosen).

Further, Escobar (1995) explains how the construction of "the economy as an autonomous domain" (p. 60) is one important aspect in the establishment of dominant societal ways of thinking, speaking, and acting that privilege the notion of free markets and production. Social life was separated into components that were assigned laws; Westerners came to accept the so-called truth of the existence of those domains without question. Political economy—or the structuring of thought around production, labor, and markets—became the dominant code of signification.

> Simply put, modern people came to see life in general through the lens of production. Many aspects of life became increasingly economized, including human biology, the nonhuman natural world,

relations among people, and relations between people and nature. The langauges of everyday life became entirely pervaded by the discourses of production and the market. (Escobar, 1995, p. 60)

Feminist scholars have illustrated the limits of and problems with capitalism in relation to women's lives. As an example, Dunaway (2002) outlined how dominant capitalist modes of functioning have created discourses that do not sufficiently recognize the work of women. Living within these modes, families are often viewed and interpreted as "households" or units that pool income. However, most of the world's households acquire only "a minority of their survival needs from wages" (p. 130; Wallerstein, 1983), products, or markets. Resources brought by women (like their own bodies and specialized life knowledges) are not included within capitalist definitions of how households functions. Further, women's functioning around the world has not included major capitalist constructs. An example of this contradiction is the capitalist notion of commodity chain, a network of labor that ends in a finished product. Much analysis has been devoted to the factors that influence this chain and how its products can be disseminated. In contrast, however, feminist scholars have illustrated that a characteristic of much of the work that women have historically been allowed or encouraged to do lacks any type of "finished" product (e.g., infant care, elder care, housecleaning).

Imperialist perspectives and impositions have obviously been influenced by and even perpetuated capitalism; there are scholars and others who would even propose that imperialism and capitalism produce and reproduce each other, one making the existence of the other possible. From the extraction of resources in conquered lands, to the imposition of market economies around the world through organizations like the World Bank and constructs like sustainable development, to actions (however informal in appearance) that are taken by countries like the United States to maintain economic interests in "foreign" lands, capitalism and imperialism are certainly intertwined. The great inescapable has permeated our lives. We seriously doubt that elimination of capitalism is possible. After all, the grand narratives of power that have invaded us previously, specifically religion and science, have not disappeared, and even though we would critique, deconstruct, and wish to reconceptualize them, we would probably support components of capitalist economic perspectives. However, we agree with Foucault that everything is dangerous, and believe that capitalism and its ties with imperialism have long passed the point of extreme danger. The two are now combined to interpret all aspects of our lives, to judge and legitimate actions both locally and globally, and to silence entirely voices that have been removed (whether physically, though dominant discourses, or denial of capital) from the capitalist world system. Continued public postcolonial critique and reconceptualizations are absolutely necessary.

First, Second, Third, and Fourth Worlds. The notion of dividing the world into hierarchical categories has literally been created by the first world, is generally associated with amounts of industrial development and economic power, and is actually repulsive to us. We, therefore, avoid the use of the terms with the exception of usage that we believe illustrates the way language is invoked to imply superiority or inferiority, to oppress or create power. It was our intent to use the terms in ways that remind the reader of the Western notion of superiority and ways that these notions insult and degrade.

Recent work in the field of psychology illustrates this unquestioned categorization of others, even based on country of origin. Moghaddam (1987) discusses psychology's three world's by representing the United States as the first, Western Europe and the Soviet Union as the second (although we would guess that currently some former Soviet countries would be labeled third world), and Africa, Asia, and Latin America as the third. The so-called third world is represented as ignorant, uneducated, having problems, and needy (Mohanty, 1991). This construction of an inferior world, a third world, represents a certain Western perspective that would create power over particular peoples by universalizing and homogenizing (Escobar, 1995). Additionally, minorities in industrialized countries like the U.S. have been labeled fourth world (Young, 2001). A discourse is created that justifies imperialist beliefs and actions over others (Bhabha, 1990). In short, often hyphenated phrases, many of the world's people are labeled and minimized as "not as good, smart, civilized, or advanced" as the rest of us.

Development and Sustainability. Development theory emerged during the years between the two world wars and incorporated the assumptions that postcolonial nations should be transformed into modern industrial states, and that economic growth would occur in linear stages toward the "advanced" state exhibited by the first world. This model has been widely critiqued as (1) ignoring biased Western assumptions (Escobar, 1995; Havinden & Meredith, 1993; Mehmet, 1995; Rostow, 1960; Weiner, 1966), (2) facilitating the practice of purposeful underdevelopment (Amin, 1974, 1977, 1988; Cardoso & Faletto, 1979; Frank, 1969; Furtado, 1964; Rodney, 1989), and (3) fostering the construction of inequitable capitalist accumulation by those countries already labeled advanced in the name of world market needs (Bukharin, 1972; Lenin, 1965 [1917]; Wallerstein, 1979, 1984). Some economists continue to apply this notion of development that mirrors the Enlightenment Eurocentric assumption that all races and cultures are progressing toward enlightened reason (Hadjor, 1993; Tucker, 1999). Different nations are assumed to be at different levels on the hierarchical continuum.

In recent years, inspired by various social struggles such as the women's and ecological movements, a postdevelopment theory has emerged that recognizes agency and emphasizes such constructs as cultural pluralism, human rights within the context of cultural analysis, self-reliance, and sustainability (Alvarez, Dagnino, & Escobar, 1998; Munck & O'Hearn, 1999; Waterman, 1998). Escobar (1995), however, explains how the discourse of sustainable development is actually a relegitimation and reinscription of development theory with a redistribution of arguments.

The notion of sustainable development would be to eliminate poverty and protect the environment from within a Western rational. The idea is that the life-threatening, fragility of the earth "must be recognized—and managed" (World Commission on Environment & Development, 1987, p. 1). According to Escobar (1995), scientists and businesspeople have joined to create the notion of sustainable development that attempts to legitimate the management of people all over the earth. The discourse appears to integrate environmentalism and concern for nature and survival with management and industrialization. However, the reinscription of the old Western, developmental control apparatus is clear. First, sustainable development is part of a larger discourse of global environmentalism that does not always recognize the overuse of resources by those who continue to dominate and the inequitable burden placed on those identified as the other (e.g., poor, third world, developing). Second, activities of poor people around the world are increasingly blamed for environmental problems without recognizing the ways that physical and economic imperialism has required that indigenous and colonized peoples pressure the environment simply for their own survival. This blaming also shifts responsibility from the global industrial complex. Third, the construct of sustainable development appears to reconcile two old conflicts—economic growth and the environment—by creating poverty as the new enemy of the environment. The real message of sustainability is that "it is growth (read: capitalist market expansion), and not the environment, that has to be sustained" (Escobar, 1995, p. 195). Managing the environment is a "panacea" (p. 196) for sustaining market growth. Finally, the discourse constructs nature as environment, as an indispensable resource to the industrial system and the human agent. The economic worldview is actually reinscribed onto ecological perspectives, for example, finding more efficient uses for resources. Nature is reconstituted as controllable, and management of both the environment and others by those in power (e.g., Western scientists, businesspeople) is again legitimated. This movement is a massive attempt toward "the reinscription of the Earth into capital via the gaze of science" (p. 202).

Border Knowledges and Hybridity

Postcolonial critiques have attempted to recognize the complexity of life through such notions as border lives, hybridity, and transcultural/transnational existances. Imperialism, whether physical or economic, leads to both the creation of boundaries or borders between people(s) and the crossing of those borders. Cultures intersect or even clash—national boundaries are crossed and at times shattered as people live on the geographic divides between nations—languages clash and at times even join forces to form unthought-of communications—individuals from different racial backgrounds, cultures, and experiences join their lives together.

Anzaldua (1987) defines the borderlands as "wherever two or more cultures edge each other, where people of different races occupy the same territory" (p. 1). Although this definition would appear to have an element of romanticism, Anzaldua is quick to further explain that there should be no illusion why borders are created. The purpose is to separate the safe from the unsafe, to separate us from them. However, the ultimate goal, separation, is never quite achieved. Those who inhabit the borders are thought of as the "squint-eyed, the perverse, the queer, the troublesome, the mongrel, the mulatto, the half-bread, the half-dead: in short those who cross over, pass over, or go through the confines of the 'normal'" (p. 25). The collision of cultures in the margin both reestablishes the borders and contests them, as contact challenges the notions of binary racialized, gendered, or ethnic opposites. The border is never a place of peace but always under contestation, always ambivalent and confused. Stoler (1992) has described the border as an internal frontier, always being created and always decomposing. The border is contested physically and as regarding origin (De Alva, 1995). For the colonizers, borders are essential as part of the process of fixing and ordering social sectors, especially the more rebellious ones. For subalterns (the colonized), borders are locations where people come together to resist overtly and covertly.

Cradled in one culture, sandwiched between two cultures, straddling all three cultures, and their value systems, *la mestiza* undergoes a struggle of flesh, a struggle of borders, an inner war. Like all people, we perceive the version of reality that our culture communicates. Like others having or living in more than one culture, we get multiple often opposing messages. The coming together of two self-consistent but habitually incompatible frames of reference causes un choque, a cultural collision. (Anzaldua, 1987, p. 100)

Border messages have been communicated through the construction of the term hybrid. As a concept, hybridity was generally used to invoke images of the border as a place where the negative consequences of racial encounters played out (Papastergiadis, 2000). Even when the scientific bases of racism (which created hybridity as something monstrous) were discredited, the negative images persisted. More recently, however, hybridity has become more popular as so-called hybrids have taken on essentialist models of identity and turned them upside down. "The most positive feature of hybridity is that it invariably acknowledges that identity is constructed though a negotiation of difference, and that the presence of fissures, gaps and contradictions is not necessarily a sign of failure" (p. 170).

As all of these perspectives would suggest, there can be no one unified understanding of what border or margin means. However, what does seem to be common is an experience of ambiguity and multiple consciousness. Thus, border knowledges, wherever derived, involve a tolerance for ambiguity and reconciling seemingly contradictory points of view into a whole. This ambivalence actually becomes a place of strength from which la mestiza creates new consciousness and new realities. Given the extent of colonialism around the world, the future belongs to the mestiza (Anzaldua, 1987). "The mestizos, the mulattos and their mixtures, coming into their own in this century as political forces, have brought to the fore the fundamental question of the nature of colonialism and postcolonialism as categories/practices of contestation" (De Alva, 1995, p. 244). Direct challenges to imperialist-assumed superiority and power can be generated from the standpoint or political location of border/hybrid lives (Harding, 1998; Papastergiadis, 2000).

CREATING POSSIBILITIES FOR DECOLONIALIZING

The purpose of this book is to generate decolonial possibilities, yet the term is probably the most difficult to define. An expected definition would be that people who have been physically taken-over, controlled, and occupied would gain control over their own lives. However, the notion is much more complex. We have already introduced economic and political colonization, as well as constructions of hierarchy and privilege as found in patriarchy. In future chapters, we discuss ways that disciplinary knowledge colonizes, and how networks of power dictate how people view themselves, all basically tied to Western expansion and the Enlightenment/modernist projects that legitimated this expansion. Can one talk about "undoing" these forms of colonization and imperialism? Or must new ways of being be generated? We hope that the information and perspectives that we present in this book will provide opportunities for decolonialist understanding and actions.

The critical avoidance of the construction of power over others is not always about rejecting or discarding Western thought (Chakrabarty, 2000), nor is it necessarily about some type of postcolonial revenge (Gandhi, 1998). Rather, decolonization is about recognizing how dominant, established ways of knowing are at the same time "indispensable and inadequate," and how this kind of thought can be "renewed from and for the margins" (Chakrabarty, 2000, p. 16). Further, decolonization is about possibilities for liberation from the range of locations that we inhabit, from the unthought of recesses of our beings, and from our collective will to hear, see, and respect the multiplicity of lives that inhabit our world.

2
COLONIALIST INFLUENCE
Constituting Realms of Power

Colonialism reshaped existing structures of human knowledge. No branch of learning was left untouched ... like the functioning of ideology itself, simultaneously a misrepresentation of reality and its reordering

—Loomba, 1998, p. 57

In this chapter we turn our focus to the rise of rationalism and how it changed the ways in which the Western world conceived of thought, to the realms of unquestioned power that were created by the West. Imperialism emerged from that time in European history known as the Enlightenment, the period know for philosophical perspectives that fostered logic, truth orientations, and the belief in progress, science, and rational thought. Although the Enlightenment is not commonly regarded as a colonialist project, imperialism might be one of its longest lasting legacies (Smith, 1999). The Enlightenment signaled the end of such irrational ways of functioning as feudalism and superstitious values while introducing beliefs in progress, science, free inquiry, and rational thinking (Chakrabarty, 2000), most often referred to as the project of modernity. This project was focused and continues to focus on the individual and the capacity for reason functioning within a society that "promotes individual autonomy and self-interest, and on a state which has a rational rule of law which regulates a public sphere of life, but which allows individuals to pursue their economic self interest" (Smith, 1999, p. 59).

This capacity for reason and rationalism was seen as a weapon against premodern ways of thinking. Mbembe (2001) describes the characteristics of traditional African societies before the advent of colonialism, pointing out the traits that made them so irresistible to the modernist project. Traditional societies were characterized by facticity and arbitrariness; the construction of "time" as stationary and a strong resistance to change, and person predominance over notions of the individual. Facticity is a term used by Hegel to explain why a thing exists; things simply are, have always been, and need no further explanation. Arbitrariness is a characteristic of societies in which "myth and fable denote order and time" (Mbembe, 2001 p. 4). Such supposedly illogical explanations for life collided in the most brutal way with the project of modernity. The very extent of the difference creates Africa as a special kind of "unreality," a place of absolute nothingness and abolition. Thus, according to Stoler and Cooper (1997), French colonialists justified their colonizing efforts as part of their vision of a just and socialist society that could not be attained by the simple-minded unless aided from the outside.

Said (1995) describes the Enlightenment view of the world as "mankind" forming "a marvelous almost symphonic whole whose progress and formations, again as a whole, could be studied exclusively as a concerted and secular historical experience" (p. 21). Not as widely recognized is the context within which such a view of the world became popular, a period of growing nationalism in Europe. Although the Enlightenment was supposedly a time to celebrate and recognize the accomplishments as well as the connectedness of humanity, in effect, the celebration was of one narrow view of humanity that resulted in the exclusion and even physical conquering of those who did not fit that view (creating them as the "other").

Colonialism can be seen in many ways as part of a war against the premodern, a grand project that spread the truths of reason and rationalism around the world. However, the relationship between colonialism and the project of modernity is far more complex than a simple cause-and-effect equation. The "discovery" of new lands, natural resources, and peoples provided not only commercial fodder in terms of resources for the colonialist powers to exploit, but also material for the honing of such scientific processes as systems of representation and classification of natural resources. The fact that there were many indigenous contributions to "new" knowledges was rarely recognized. There were no acknowledgments that "other people could have done things before or better than" the colonizers (Smith, 1999, p. 61). Although conquest and subjugation are not uniquely colonial experiences, the Enlightenment version of colonialism combined violence with a belief in the universal validity of such political principles as the need for a rational form of government, opening the door for fierce debates as to what that kind of government should be, who would be in control, and who could be a citizen.

The intersection between modernism and colonialism was also marked by a massive process of renaming (Smith, 1999). For example, collecting objects, whether natural species or "rare treasures," became a hobby for many Europeans during this time. Smith sees collecting as renaming the process of stealing. Collecting was portrayed as a process of rescuing precious things from decay and destruction, an explanation that neatly glosses over the processes of exploitation and thievery they in fact represented. The genocide that caused massive destruction of indigenous populations on many continents, but most of all in the United States, was conveniently renamed the survival of the fittest, a scientific concept that reinforced the idea that native populations died out due to their own genetic inferiority rather than through systematic extermination. Similarly, Stoler and Cooper (1997) have remarked on the enormous bureaucratic structures that colonialism put into place, which occupied itself with "classifying people and their attributes, with censuses and surveys and ethnographies, with recording transactions, marking space, establishing routines and standardizing practices" (p. 11). Chakrabarty (2000) has also commented on how one of the by-products of modernism was to further disempower women, as what have been seen as traditional women's knowledges did not stand up to the test of rationalism.

Colonialist knowledges, discourses, and ways of interpreting the world were imposed as if they were truths that could not be questioned. These "knowledges" have included a vast range of everything from definitions of human beings and what "it means to be human," to universalist interpretations of language and literacy, to beliefs about gender, time, and space. Further, categorizations of knowledge emerged from the Enlightenment into so-call disciplines, as if the categorizations were truths that explained chunks of reality that should be discovered and known by universal "man." These knowledges were imposed on the colonized and continue to be imposed on all of us with the assumptions that origin, bias, and limitations are not issues. The purpose of this chapter is to reveal the realms of colonialist power hidden in the knowledges that dominate our world today. We also demonstrate ways that these knowledges may be further critiqued by using feminist methodology.

POSTCOLONIAL CRITIQUE AND CHALLENGES TO ACCEPTED KNOWLEDGE DISCOURSES

This section focuses on how what Powell and Frankenstein (1997) call "false facts" became part of our "taken for granted knowledge" about the world (p. 1). As an example they quote from Grossman (1994):

Geographically, Europe does not exist, since it is only a peninsula on the vast Eurasian continent. Europe has always been a political and cultural definition.... Before the 19th century, geographers generally referred to it as "Christendom." When colonialism began to spread Western culture and religion to all corners of the globe, some British and German geographers began to delineate the eastern boundaries of a European continent. What they were actually doing was trying to draw the eastern limits of "Western civilization" and the white race. (p. 39)

Yet this so-called false fact of Europe (and some of its former colonies) has constituted itself not only into a geographic reality but also into the intellectual center of the earth. As we discuss dominant discourses (or realms of power) like humanity, language/literacy, gender, or time, we ask: How do false facts become accepted as reality, and even constituted as a reality to be imposed on everyone? Who perpetuates these imperialist notions? What are their agendas?

Humanity: Fact or Fiction?

Increasingly, we face narrower definitions of what it means to be a human being or person. The quality of humanness or humanity, for lack of better words, has come to be defined essentially by Eurowestern male Christian values. As Lorde (1997) emphasizes, history conditions many of us to see human beings in "simplistic opposition to one another: dominant/subordinate, good/bad, up/down, superior/inferior" (p. 374). Other dominant beliefs include such notions as all human beings are created with potential and it is human to want to make full use of this potential or to help others do so; human beings are monogamous and heterosexual; life, liberty, and the pursuit of happiness are universal human goals; human beings are aware of their limits; the human and divine are separate; and so forth. As Ingold (1996) states, the Enlightenment "proclaimed the triumph of human reason over a recalcitrant nature"; every person acts in "the pursuit of rational self-interest" (p. 25). A narrow model thus exists that defines what it means to be a person in the 21st century. However, there is a vast body of literature, some of it critical, that emphasizes that the definition of a human being may, above all, be cultural. We choose to begin with "humanness" or the "fact/fiction of humanity" as the first major accepted truth to question— this is, a truth that has far-reaching implications.

Humans and Nonhumans. Howell (1996) states that in much of Western philosophy human beings have been treated as if different from the rest of the environment, including animals. This separation has been justi-fied by using the Cartesian notion of separation of mind and body; further, humans are defined as superior to animals just as thinking is privileged as superior to feeling (Skultans, 1977). Prior to this dichoto-mous separation, "man thought of himself as an integral part of the world. . . . His interrelationship with nature was so intensive that he could not look at it from without; he was inside it" (as cited in Palsson, 1999, p. 65) Cartesian dualism separated humans from the "the mother-world of the Middle Ages," but compensated for that by creating the idea of the rational man with a rational ego and the ability to be objec-tive (p. 66). Thus, part of the definition of what it means to be human has been a construction of what is not human—humans are not ani-mals, humans are not part of the earth, humans are not inanimate, and so forth.

However, in an ethnographic study that Howell (1996) conducted with the Chewong, a group of Aboriginals in the Malay tropical rain forest, he found that animals and other "natural" species such as trees and plants were included in the construction of what it means to be a human or a person. The Chewong people categorized the world in terms of the presence or absence of consciousness, defined as a "sense of lan-guage, reason, intellect and moral consciousness' (p. 131). Any thing or person, be it "gibbon, human, wild pig, frog, rambutan fruit, bamboo leaf, the thunder being or a specific boulder," could be identified as having this consciousness. Furthermore, absence of consciousness did not mean automatic inclusion in another category. One of the characteristics of this culture was that schema seemed to be organized on the basis of iden-tifying and naming rather than clustering. Further, the principle that seemed to drive the schema was the foil of achieving equality rather than the construction of hierarchy.

Descola (1996) has also suggested that eastern scientific traditions are probably the only ones in which the distinctions between humans and nonhumans are most rigid and clearly defined. In many other contexts, the differences are more likely to be expressed contextually rather than systematically. There are differences in the ways in which societies orga-nize knowledge. To illustrate, Western intellectual traditions (also called totemic systems by Descola) are shaped by a need to organize units into hierarchies; whereas in other intellectual traditions (called animic tradi-tions by Descola), the emphasis may be more on looking at the commonalities between humans and other natural species. Examples of animism include the cosmology of the Tukanoan Indians of Colombia who live by a principle of reciprocity, which insists that humans and non-humans must share the biosphere equally. Patterns of life within some societies are based on the belief that the amount of energy in the cosmos is fixed, and therefore, humans must return to nonhumans the energy used up while hunting for food. This energy reciprocity is believed to be accomplished as humans revert to being animals after death. Humans and animals are therefore seen as interchangeable. Descola also points out that in cultures like the Jivaroan tribes of eastern Ecuador, nonhumans are also considered persons, when linked by ties of living together (such as domesticated plants) and affinity (such as forest animals).

Human Rights and Values. Another sweeping generalization that is made about human beings is that everyone deserves the same "rights," as there are human universals that all people value and deserve. Whether all human beings would conceive of the same rights, or agree on what they value, is debatable.

Documents such as the UN "Universal" Declaration of Human Rights, which is accepted by many countries, are seen as evidence that a basic charter of rights exists, of which all human beings are guaranteed. According to Haraway (1989), only 8 of the 56 countries that were then a part of the United Nations did not support this declaration, 6 of which were communist countries. Their viewpoint was that economic, cultural and social rights were just as important as individual rights. As Bulbeck (1998) has shown, such declarations do little to address systematic inequities that limit the lives of many people far more than any denial of these basic rights. For example, for many working-class women, freely choosing low paying jobs is a twistedly ironic interpretation of the individual right to work.

Bulbeck (1998) also critiques the UN Declaration as applying mostly to men. For example, violence against women was not initially defined as an act of torture and was thus not considered as a violation of human rights. This was, however, later rectified by the United Nations. Efforts such as a meeting of over 600 Asian and Pacific women to propose a new definition of democracy highlight the diverse ways in which the concept of rights can be viewed. For these women, democracy was defined not as a system of government but as a way in which people relate to one another. The concept of rights has also been seen as violating the very important concept of harmony (Cheung, 1989).

For many countries in which the concept of the individual did not really exist as in the Western definition, signing the Declaration was an empty act. Spring (2001) has looked at the whole question of universal human rights, recognizing a growing discomfort with the idea that the West is both creator and protector of the idea of universal human rights. Spring quotes the work of Onuma (Onuma, 1999), who denounces the hypocrisy inherent in such ideas:

For those who have experienced colonial rule and interventions under such beautiful slogans as "humanity" and "civilization" the term human rights looks like nothing more than another beautiful slogan by which great powers rationalize their interventionist policies. (p. 119)

Onuma reminds us that it is actually difficult to trace a human rights tradition in the West because of the long history of warfare, genocide, and colonialism. He also makes the point that the history that does exist is a history of qualifications, a history that has continued to deny women's rights and that has exhibited a continual devotion to colonialism (Spring, 2001). Puntambekar (1973) has also critiqued the Western tradition of human rights as being too grounded in reason and science and for suppressing the spiritual dimension of human life.

As all of the above perspectives would suggest, what it means to be a human being and what human beings value vary greatly according to location, history, social position, and the political agendas of those who are allowed to speak the language of human rights. To illustrate further, the attempt to present a unified set of "Christian" values as core values for all humanity is built once again on a set of binaries, as these values are defined in opposition to ways of life that do not subscribe to them. Also, the values that are put forward are often such notions as peace and democracy, highlighted as being in contrast to the supposedly warrior-like Native American cultures. Research has, however, shown that "70 percent or more of all pre-contact societies in North America practiced no form of warfare at all" (Jaimes & Halsey, 1997, p. 302), revealing fabricated false Christian or Western values that are used to create groups of people as immoral and as the "other." As an aside, Jaimes and Halsey link this functioning without war directly to the fact that many of these "traditional" societies were never dominated by males (which, we would add, may also be the reason why Western colonizers attempted to discredit them as lacking values).

Even the definitions of particular values vary across cultures, peoples, and even individuals. Castellano (2000) relates an anecdote about the hearings that were convened to decide whether it would be appropriate to stop building hydroelectric power plants in northern Quebec. One of the elders was asked to testify about Cree life and how it would be impacted by the proposed developments. When he was asked to swear that he would tell the truth, he asked the translator to explain what the word truth meant, and when it was translated as something that was always valid and applied to all people, he replied "I can't promise to tell you the truth, I can only tell you what I know" (p. 25). Obviously, the notions of humanity, humanness, human values and human rights vary greatly across cultures and peoples, as well as across social and historical contexts, power orientations, and political agendas.

Language and Literacy

Language is the human behavior perhaps more deeply accepted as a truth than any other. A world without language, or human beings who do not use language, is considered impossible by most people. However, as many postcolonial scholars have pointed out, language has been pivotal in the continuing colonization of the world by Euro-Americans (Gandhi, 1998; Loomba, 1998; Viruru, 2001). Language has been used as a critical dividing factor to distinguish between "civilization and barbarism" (Seed, 1991): those civilizations that use written languages are considered superior to those who do not (p. 8). Gandhi (1998) maintains that language or text, more than any other behavior, is one of the most "significant instigators and purveyors of colonial power" (p. 141). Tiffin and Lawson (1994) state that although colonial power was originally enforced through "guns, guile and disease" (p. 3), it was maintained through means such as language. Language is seen by many as a behavior that shapes and creates cultures and that has been used to further the political ends of colonial powers.

Britton's (1999) explanation of the postcolonial theory of Edouard Glissant focuses particularly on the issue of language and how it is related to ways of viewing the world. According to Glissant, Western cultures are particularly "essentialist" in that they insist upon reducing both people and ideas to an essence. In contrast, Glissant puts forth the concept of "Relation": a way in which different cultures and people might interact with one another. Relation is an antiimperialist project that Britton characterizes as a connection that fosters "equality and respect for the Other as different from oneself" (p. 11). Set up to counteract Western humanism's relentless quest to define and limit the "other" permanently, the concept of the "Relation" sees the "other" not only as equal, but as needed precisely because of the difference. The foundational idea, therefore, is one of diversity rather than fixed properties. Glissant characterizes most Western languages as languages of essence that contribute to the relentless essentialism that characterizes colonialism.

Individuals and cultures that exist in "relation" to one another are also seen as accepting the idea that the other person or culture has a right to be "opaque." Opacity is considered a necessary condition for relationships to flourish, "the more the Other resists in his thickness or fluidity (without restricting himself to that) the more expressive his reality becomes and the more fruitful the relationship becomes" (Britton, 1999, p. 18). Opacity is thus seen as a fundamental right, as it is a way in which human beings can resist being categorized and essentialized. It is also a way of resisting what Glissant sees as a particularly colonializing concept: "understanding," especially when one recognizes that the root of the French word for understanding (*comprende*) is the word *prendre*, which means to take.

> If we look at the process of understanding beings and ideas as it operates in Western society, we find that it is founded on an insistence on this kind of transparency. In order to "understand" and therefore accept you, I must reduce your density to this scale of conceptual measurement which gives me a basis for comparisons and perhaps for judgements. (as cited in Britton, 1999, p. 19)

Western ways of using language, according to Glissant, both comply with and further this essentialist view of understanding.

The Will to Literacy. Closely related to the issue of language is that of literacy, which is seen by many as another essential truth. The position is that literate human beings are always better off than illiterate ones. The images of illiteracy are often those of people of color behind bars (Kozol, 1991; Rockhill, 1993; Stuckey, 1991). Yet as a growing body on critical literacy has shown, literacy is another false fact created in a particular social and political contexts in which it is valued; however, human beings have functioned very successfully in a range of times and cultures without being literate.

Graff (2001) conducted an analysis of the history of literacy, especially as it relates to the ways in which it has been taught to children. He distinguishes three basic strands as playing an important role in defining what literacy is, each of which has been given importance at different times in history: (1) elementary or basic literacy, levels of which are currently "scientifically" measured by standardized tests; (2) an association with certain clearly defined moral and personal characteristics and conditions of civilization (e.g., morality, order, democracy, progress, and productivity); and (3) new literacies like scientific and technological literacies, cultural literacy, and now also "emotional, moral, environmental, television and food literacies" (p. 7). As the diversity of these three strands would indicate, defining what literacy is becomes difficult if not impossible, "an exceptionally slippery subject and object" (p. 8). Further, literacy is invested with an enormous range of assumptions and presumptions. Graff's historical analysis of these three strands led him to draw a series of what he calls lessons about literacy as a concept:

1. Contemporary literacy constructs and practices are historically resistant to change.
2. The complexity of literacy is not well recognized. A simplistic construction of literacy as a human right further oversimplifies the construct, leading to such simple and colonialist binaries as literate-illiterate; written-oral and civilized-barbaric.
3. Literacy is often presumed to be value-neutral or if ascribed a value, it is overwhelmingly "good."
4. "More than excessive are the damages, the massive human costs in domains developed and undeveloped that follow from the long domination of theoretical presumptions that elevate the literate, the written as opposed to the nonliterate, to the power and status of the dominant partner in what has been called call the *great dichotomy*" (Graff, 2001, p. 16). Graff sees this as an instance of the arrogance of the West in privileging the "technology of the intellect" over the human spirit.
5. Learning literacy is hard work and usually takes place when it is needed in real life.
6. There are multiple ways in which human beings can become literate, yet universal public schooling functions as though the process is simple and the methods are definable.
7. The compulsory inclusion of literacy in most schools is a form of "foundationalism" (p. 19), presuming that given the right conditions simple abilities to read and write will develop in children and that those abilities in themselves are the foundation to a better life.
8. There is no one simple route to achieving literacy, whereas in the late 20th and early 21st centuries, there has been an assumption that economic development is directly linked to investing in systems of formal education.

Reading and Colonization. To further illustrate the complex roots of literacy, Luke and Freebody (1997) have examined the relationship between reading and colonization and conclude that the ways in which reading was taught for many centuries, both in the margins and in the centers, quite explicitly defined who belonged to the center and the margins. In the colonies in particular, the goal of literacy education was to specifically introduce classical English literature, but with a twist. Access to the higher levels of this kind of education was limited to mostly urban middle-class males. Even women who did well in this system were barred after a certain point. Thus, according to Luke and Freebody, for most of the 19th and the early parts of the 20th centuries, reading instruction was based on a two-stage model. The first stage included such basics as word recognition, handwriting, and spelling; whereas the second stage revolved around the classics, being limited to only a few. In Australia, for example, the Aboriginal, Asian, and Islander populations were rarely allowed to access the second stage of literacy. The materials used to teach reading during this period were quite explicitly related to colonial interests (for example, using reading textbooks called the *Royal Readers*). In the 1950s in Australia, such readers were replaced with other reading materials that emphasized the values of Western suburban life. However, the skills that were emphasized in the readers continued to be quite similar: word recognition, letter to sound correspondence, and spelling. Luke and Freebody see this pattern as illustrative; changing the content of the readers and not the skills creates an image of reading that is value-free and neutral. Setting up reading as essentially decontextualized also reifies the image of learners as individuals with sets of predefined (Western and normative) capacities. This kind of reader "is not well fitted to a rural economic or colonial experience but rather to a more urban industrialized experience, and an experience by which the standardization of apparently every day suburban life is the core of what would emerge later as a globalized set of cultural patterns' (p. 189). The replacement of explicitly colonial readers with new heroes like Dick and Jane (who have subtly controlled racialized and gendered identities) was in some ways a move from the colonial to the neocolonial. Language and literacy have certainly been used to contribute to the larger project of colonizing minds, intellects, and emotions, creating desires to think like and be like the Empire.

Gender

The creation of a particular image of what it means to be a woman is one of colonialism's most powerful influences on the world as we know it today. This image so dominates that many continue to believe that the notion of gender as socially constructed is ridiculous, as gender is supposedly only a biological difference. However, as Mohanty (1991) argues, the things that bind women together are not based on biological similarities, but on what she calls "secondary sociological and anthropological universals" (p. 259). Only recently has gender come to be seen as not just a property that human beings possess, but as inexplicably tied to social structure (Harding, 1998).

The possibility that gender is socially constructed creates avenues for the examination of supposedly gender neutral or natural actions, for example, the notion that the third world development policies are (masculine) gendered. Bulbeck (1998) has also shown how modernization changed the ways in which gender roles were defined in many Western societies. Before the Industrial Revolution, women actually had many more rights, like the right to own property and to be members of parliament. Clear-cut distinctions between genders only came later in history.

Stoler (1997) demonstrates that gender inequities were an integral part of colonial logic, and that sexual control was a key feature in the establishment of colonial rule in many parts of the world. European colonizers soon found that separating the colonizers from the colonized was not as easy a distinction as might be imagined. As different parts of the globe became places where imperial powers vied with one another for control and multiple criteria for defining who was or was not part of the elite emerged, the regulation of sexual and domestic contact between people grew increasingly important. Said (1978) has shown how the logic that created orientalism was essentially gendered; the submission and possession of oriental women by European men came to symbolize the subjugation of the orient by the occident. A strident misogyny has been displayed throughout the various constructions of Empire.

On a more obvious physical level was the question of who "bedded and wedded" with whom, which became strictly regulated according to the interests of the various colonial empires. For several centuries, "the sexual sanctions and conjugal prohibitions of colonial agents were rigorously debated and carefully codified" (Stoler, 1997, p. 347). Through imposing restrictions on European women's access to the colonies and not employing married males, colonial powers in effect created the system of concubinage (a colonized woman living with a European man), which was the most common domestic arrangement in the colonies until the early 20th century. This arrangement also limited prostitution and the attendant dangers of diseases like syphilis, considered a threat to that primary colonial instrument, the European man. European women were discouraged from living in the colonies, even after colonies were considered stable and safe places. All of these policies created conditions under which populations and privileges could be more easily regulated.

Discourses of racial difference (and superiority) have also been predicated on beliefs about gender; racism and sexism have become so intertwined that they are impossible to separate (Stepan, 1982). Examples include colonial scientific studies that drew parallels between the skulls of native women and infants, and compared males from the "lower races" to European women. As colonial conquests increasingly included the conquests of women of color, the whiteness of White middle-class women came to stand more and more for purity and White male superiority in the name of protection (Bulbeck, 1998).

A primary target for colonial power was the status held by women in indigenous societies (Jaimes & Halsey, 1997). Jesuit priests attempted to teach Native American cultures about the principle of obedience to males that women were expected to follow (Leacock, 1981). Other actions, such as the colonizers' demands to trade only with men and educating "native" men in Western ways were explicitly designed to alter the balance of power within these cultures. None of the more than 300 treaties between the U.S. government and multiple indigenous nations included the participation of women, because males in the U.S. government insisted on dealing only with men (Jaimes & Halsey, 1997).

Even the impact of more female-friendly discourses like Western feminist scholarship has not always been positive. Mohanty (1991) charges that Western feminist scholarship in fact served in many ways to reify the identity of women from the third world. The first wave of Western feminist discourse assumed that "women" were an already constituted group of people, with identical interests and desires, regardless of the multiple locations from which they came. This assumed homogeneity lends itself to the creation of stereotypes that haunt third world women who are often automatically assumed to be sexually less "free" than women in the West, as well as "ignorant, poor, uneducated, tradition bound, domestic, family oriented and victimized" (p. 258). Such a discourse does not leave room for assertions such as that of Jaimes and Halsey (1997) that Native American women, "contrary to those images of meekness, docility and subordination to males ... [h]ave formed the very core of indigenous resistance to genocide and colonization since the first moment of conflict between Indians and invaders" (p. 298). As these authors also point out, whereas in the United States it is only just becoming acceptable for women to take part in wars, Native American women did so many centuries ago, particularly after the European invasion of North America. Furthermore, many precontact Native American societies were matrilineal, and, in contrast to the hegemonic masculinity of the Judeo-Christian traditions they later encountered, their religious cosmologies had many feminine elements.

Gender is a false truth that has been used by some European and American males (and others who accept the notions as beyond question) to impose patriarchy, racism, and control on indigenous and other colonized peoples. In many of those colonized societies, women played equal roles, yet imperialism (1) constructed a regulatory system over sexual behavior and attempted to change cultural beliefs about women;

(2) eliminated women when possible from negotiations across cultures and nations; and (3) imposed an invasive misogynous world vision that is, even today, not often challenged.

Time

Spivak (1999) provides an interesting analysis of the ways in which the concept of time has come to dominate European thought and ways of being. Kant was responsible for the prevalent idea within European thought that nothing could be, think, or act outside the framework of time. Thus, to Kant, human life could not exist outside temporal boundaries. This insistence on the existence of time as an absolute sequential entity gave rise to the ways in which we commonly view the complexity of human life; even though human existence is incredibly diverse, it is still seen as operating one temporal plane (Spivak, 1999). Time has been constructed as an absolute common thread that runs through all existence. Spivak refers to this interpretation as timing. What timing leaves out is the feeling for life and history, which is such an essential part of human existence. When all of history and reality are placed upon a diagram or graph, which is what the process of time does, the assumption is that everything has been included, that there is nothing the graph omits.

Debates about the social construction of time are not new; anthropological studies have long recognized that time is constructed differently by groups of human beings (Geertz, 1973). The Western sense of time is marked by its dependence on the instruments that are used to measure it, and the instruments themselves result from a need to know certain kinds of things; what is not universal is the need to know. Time can be looked at in a variety of ways; for example, "American" time or monochronic times, which emphasizes scheduling, blocks or periods, and beginnings/endings, or polychronic time, more characteristic of Latin America and the Middle East, which focuses on multiple events/tasks happening at one time (Milburn, 2001).

Linear conceptions of time, such as are employed in writing about history, are as empty as a bottomless sack in which events are placed. Time's "existence is independent of such events and in a sense exists prior to them. Events happen in time but time is not affected by them" (Chakrabarty, 2000, p. 73). Time is not treated as a cultural code of representation but as something that belongs to the world of absolute realities. Thus, social scientists, particularly historians, assume that everything, including people, places, and objects, can be seen as living according to time, irrespective of their own culture's ideas about what time is (or is not). "Contrary to what they themselves may have thought and however they may have organized their memories, the historian has the capacity to put them into a time we are all supposed to have shared, consciously or not" (p. 74).

For many whose history is colonialism, history is not about time but about myth or the "partial recall of the race" (Walcott, 1995, p. 370). For slaves, time was about amnesia and that amnesia, is the history the world has yet to acknowledge; to accept time is to accept the colonizer's logic:

> I say to the ancestor who sold me, and to the ancestor who bought me, I have no father, I want no such father, although I can understand you, black ghost, white ghost, when you both whisper "history," for if I attempt to forgive you both I am falling into your idea of history which justifies, explains and expiates. (p. 370)

Mbembe (2001) describes a "time of African existence" as "neither a linear time nor a simple sequence in which each moment effaces, annuls and replaces those that preceded it," but as a concept that is fraught with multiplicities. Rather than viewing time as one single entity, Mbembe conceptualizes it as a coming together of many forces, so that any one moment is actually a combination of the past, present, and future. Mbembe also defines temporality as subjectivity, suggesting that people's life worlds are defined not by some abstract way of measurement called time but through the ways in which they construct existence. Any moment in time, if looked at through the lens of subjectivity, is filled with multiple complex relationships and events, "of discontinuities and reversals, inertias and swings that overlay one another, interpenetrate one another and envelope one another," and to define it in isolation from its context is to commit once again an act of colonization (p. 14).

Related to the concept of time, as some feminist theorists have illustrated, is the concept of space. The ways in which the two are seen as dichotomous is also seen as an "imperialist" way of knowing. Space is often defined as in opposition to time, as a place where time can act. This space/time dualism has been seen as linked to the whole question of gender relations; space and women are seen as the arenas where dynamic forces such as time (seen as masculine) play themselves out (Papastergiadis, 2000). McClintock (1997) has examined how the concept of time has been used to invoke ideas of nationalism, which is seen as an ideal concept that blends the traditions of the past into the identities and cultures of the present. Further, industrial capitalism, which relies heavily on the mapping of progress, requires that one constantly reinforce the idea of the past as "archaic" regarding production and markets, in contrast to the present, which is full of novelties. This tension between the values of the past, the present, and the future is often resolved by representing time as a "natural division of *gender*" (p. 92). Women are represented as those who are "inert, backward looking and natural," as opposed to men who represent forwardness and progress. Feminist critiques of linear time have also focused on the inability of the construct to render an accurate picture of the activities that women do. Through surveys of rural women in St. Lucia, Szebo, and Cebotarev, (1990) show that 76% of the household tasks that women did were what are called "multitask": for women who cook, nurse a baby, and braid an older child's hair at the same time, time is not an accurate measure of their lives. Similar studies of domestic work in the United States have shown that for many women, multitasking is extremely common. Thus, for many women the dimension through which their lives are defined is not linear time but work-intensification.

Chakrabarty (2000) makes the point that the proper use of time was a major feature of the civilizing discourses that form such an important part of the imperialist project. Colonized peoples were given the message that knowing how to use time properly was one of the hallmarks of modernity: working, eating, playing, nursing all had to be done at the right time. Thus, according to a Bengali text written in 1887 on domestic life, "it is absolutely essential that there is a clock in every house and that ... the women are taught to read it" (as cited in Chakrabarty, 2000, p. 378). Further, evolutionary progress was also represented as a series of stages in time, from the "childhood" of the so-called primitive peoples to the "enlightened adulthood" of European imperialism (McClintock, 1997, p. 92). Insisting upon the universality of the experience of time marginalizes other ways of looking at the world. The notion of universal time also fits an advanced capitalism (Chakrabarty, 2000). Workers in advanced capitalist societies have "no option but to shed precapitalist habits of work and 'internalize' work discipline" (Thompson, 1963 as cited in Chakrabarty, 2000, p. 48). This time discipline is seen as one of the characteristics that divides the third from the first world.

THE CONSTRUCTION OF ACADEMIC DISCIPLINES

Academic knowledges are organized around the idea of disciplines and these in turn "are deeply implicated in each other and share genealogical foundations in various classical and Enlightenment philosophies" (Smith, 1999, p. 65). Most disciplines taught in universities continue to be grounded in the concept of science as a basic way of understanding the world and do not accommodate other ways of knowing. Smith suggests that whether acknowledged or not, many academic disciplines are implicated in the process of colonialism, whether through taking over "indigenous" methods or testing their methods in the colonies.

In his essay "Secular Interpretation, the Geographical Element and the Methodology of Imperialism," Said (1995) makes a case for the need to look more carefully at what we call academic disciplines and examine their creation and proliferation in light of the realities of colonialism. The development of disciplinary thinking and colonialism possess striking similarities in methodologies and intentions. Thus, we will take a deeper look at the ways in which academic disciplines have been constructed, with particular emphasis on how rationalism has shaped their constitutions.

A note of caution is also in order. As the previous sections have made clear, the extent and impact of modern colonialism is so extensive that one might say that all academic disciplines have been influenced in one way or another. A full exploration of the influence of colonialism on Western disciplinary or academic thought is, however, beyond the scope of this book. We have selected a few disciplines to briefly view in more detail. These examples have been chosen partly to represent the wide range of what constitutes disciplinary thought and partly to show the range of ways in which colonialism has impacted our thinking. We believe that each example is unique in that it reveals the multiplicity of dimensions that characterize modern capitalist, intellectual forms of colonialism.

Scientific Oversimplifications

A particularly interesting commentary on how academic disciplines have been formed has been provided by Scott (1998) in his book *Seeing Like a State*. He states, "certain forms of knowledge and control require a narrowing of vision" (p. 11). The advantages of choosing to narrow one's vision to a tunnellike state is that it simplifies complex and unwieldy realities into more manageable proportions. Narrowing one's vision brings only certain parts of reality into focus; consequently, those chosen parts are studied and measured in more detail. Eventually one forgets that the parts do not represent the whole. Scott's contention is that this kind of "tunnel vision" is fairly characteristic of states and governments and of large corporations that have very clear commercial interests and have a vested interest in controlling and manipulating knowledge about resources. Scott provides the example of the discipline of scientific forestry, established in Prussia and Saxony in the late 18th century, to illustrate this process.

Scott (1998) details how forests, although vast and complex entities, comprised of much more than trees, are seen from the angle of the state as being made up only of trees, and more specifically, as timber that might be sold for profit. All the other parts of the forests, such as the bushes and plants that have no commercial value per se, or orgamisms like grasses, ferns, and vines, which in fact keep the trees growing, are ignored. From the point of view of those in power, however, a forest is not a habitat but an economic resource to be carefully manipulated. This utilitarian view establishes its own discourse about the reality it has created; the term nature is replaced with natural resources, valued plants become crops, those that have no commercial value become weeds, valued trees are renamed as timber and others become underbrush. The state thus renames and re-creates reality. Having decided which parts of a forest were valuable and what were not, widespread efforts were put in place to grow forests that represented the state's vision of reality. Through such techniques as controlled seeding, planting, and cutting, forests were created that were comprised mainly of value-yielding trees, had little underbrush, and were easy to manage and, most important, measure. Although a fuller analysis of this example is beyond the scope of this book, the fundamental point is that powerful agencies create simplified visions of reality (driven by a need for easy control and commercial value) and then proceed to treat those visions as the only possible reality. This is analogous to the construction of the disciplines, and especially to science.

Scott (1998) also provides a detailed analysis of how systems of measurement came to be standardized and how they represent, once again, a state's attempt to order things or peoples according to its own interests. Looking in particular at the situation in France, Scott demonstrates how the implementation of the metric system of measurement was at once an act of power as well as one of cultural regulation, and how it is tied to issues that go much beyond the perceivedly simple act of measuring something. In many different cultures, measurements are done by using local standards. A common measure for string in some parts of India is the distance between thumb and elbow, as this is how it is wrapped. Ways of measuring things are thus very much grounded in local customs and practices and they are susceptible to political manipulation. For example, rather than increasing the price of a loaf of bread, the size of the loaf might be manipulated in the seller's favor. Thus, the power to define the unit of measurement is far-reaching. However, for a state to be faced with a mulitiplicity of local measurement practices, each one susceptible to local politics but also representing local ways of looking at the world, was intolerable, because the situation defied standardization and easy manipulation. In France in particular, the metric revolution was made possible by three different factors: the growth of markets that were far-flung, Enlightenment philosophy, and state enforcement of the metric system. The system thus came to represent a "rational" way to address the whole question of measurement (at once above politics and local customs). It also became a way in which to unify a country. By standardizing units of measurement, and thus reducing the ways in which local landlords could exploit the population, the metric system appeared at first glance to assure all citizens "equal rights" under the law. It was believed that the French Revolution had given the people the meter, and that it had ensured freedom for all. Conditions and context created a need for metrics; however, the results were that multiple diverse forms of measurement were eliminated.

Anthropology and Colonialism

We now turn to a much more specific discipline, anthropology, and look at how the establishment of colonial rule in many parts of the globe influenced the ways in which this discipline was constituted. According to Asad (1991), "anthropology and colonialism are both part of a much larger narrative," the restructuring of the world by European powers, to fit their vision. Although such a blunt characterization does not always do full justice to the agency and resistance adopted by human beings around the globe in resisting this change, Asad believes that European imperial dominance was an overwhelmingly "irrevocable process of transmutation" (p. 314). According to Stocking (2001), although difficult to trace the beginning of any particular phenomena, anthropology as a discipline and the cultural ideology of progress (a major force behind colonialism) were historically co-constructed.

At best, anthropology was conceived as one small piece of a larger global process, but a useful one nevertheless as its main goal was "to help classify non-European humanity in ways that would be consistent with Europe's story of triumph as progress" Asad is quick to clarify that the knowledge accumulated through anthropological inquiry did not play a major role in the spread of colonial empires because it was usually considered too context-specific to be useful in a more general sense. However, the spread of colonialism had a powerful influence on anthropology. Colonized locations and peoples became part of the "reality anthropologists sought to understand and of the way they sought to understand it" (p. 315). As Rivers (1913) explained:

> the most favorable moment for ethnographical work was from ten to thirty years after a people had been brought under the mollifying influences of the official and the missionary—long enough to ensure the friendly reception and peaceful surroundings that

were essential to such work but not long enough to have allowed any serious impairment of native culture. (as cited Stocking, 1991, p. 10)

Pers and Salemink (1999) outline what they call a threefold relationship between anthropology and colonialism: (1) Developers of anthropological processes welded power in the construction and acceptance of a particular knowledge by claiming universality for that knowledge, rather than situating it in the context in which it was produced; (2) the discourses that emerged as part of the anthropological process were entrenched within academia and elsewhere as unquestionable truths; and (3) subject peoples were "targeted by both colonial states and anthropologists as future citizens" (p. 3).

Pers and Salemink (1999) also discuss an additional point that characterizes the relationship between anthropology and colonialism—an insistence within both on certain ways of organizing perception. Modern perspectives, labeled the colonizer's religion by some, insisted on particular ways of observing and classifying the world. Seldom recognized, however, is that these ways of observation were developed through contact with many non-Western cultures. The ways of ordering the world that gave Western culture "its aura of universality" and also heavily impacted the "constitution of the anthropological subject," was "*not* produced in Europe or the West only" (p. 16). According to these scholars two concepts were a crucial part of this process—the art of travel and the art of government.

Travel, especially that involving trade, paved the way for modern colonialism, in that it was instrumental in creating the concept of nation and nationality that emerged through cross-cultural encounters. As traders were often the first to visit non-Western lands, their "mercantile" valuations of the world defined what was "normal." Works such as that of Ramus (1515–1572), which laid out a "natural method for organizing knowledge," became the basis for anthropological data collection. This approach to organizing knowledge also led to the development of such concepts as museums and statistics. The mercantile view of the world organized it essentially according to objects and their value, which also lead to the redefinition of concepts of government. As Foucault (1979) has described, government was no longer just about territory but about arrangement that would ensure the correct (based on the colonizers perception) disposition of things. Classifying possessions became part of the function of government, as well as managing populations. Enlightenment discourses strengthened these tendencies as is seen by the development of the discipline of statistics, which was developed and tested in the colonies. Thus, statistics and anthropology were not only related disciplines (as statistical accounts of populations often included details about their lives), but were also jointly pressed into service in the process of categorizing and defining diverse parts of the world (Pers & Salemink, 1999).

Bioethics: Focusing on the Individual, Losing the Human

Bioethics is described by Tong (2001) as a discipline that is based on the assumption that all human beings are similar in terms of their physical bodies, and in that they undergo similar experiences of pain and suffering. Bioethics is a way to contextualize medical experiences in light of the diversity of the world's population and the different contexts in which medicine is practiced. Although bioethics is not a feminist discipline, the field has been influenced by feminist thought. Furthermore, even though the field of bioethics is relatively new, it is still heavily influenced by Enlightenment ideas of individual personhood and autonomy (Diniz & Velez, 2001). The four foundational principles are autonomy, justice, beneficence, and nonmalefeasance (Beauchamp & Children, 1994). These principles have influenced the practice of medicine and the field of bioethics the worldwide. However, feminist theorists have questioned the assumption that the principles ensure culturally responsive healthcare, suggesting that for many women these principles themselves form a barrier toward reaching that goal. The principle of autonomy, for example, is particularly disempowering to women, actually preserving the interest of those who are already advantaged (Diniz & Velez, 2001). Feminist bioethics scholars have also questioned the very idea of universal principles as applying to that or any other field (Tong, 2001). The notion that all human beings are the same can be very dangerous because this shared "sameness" is often modeled on Euro-Western ideas of personhood (Spelman, 1988). Sameness can "operate as a tool of human oppression—of moral absolutism and colonialism" (Tong, 2001, p. 29).

A particularly interesting example of bioethics in action is given through Bergum and Bendfield's (2001) examination of the experience of pregnancy in what they call dualist and nondualist cultures. Traditional frameworks of bioethics cannot account for the life experiences of women who view the world from diverse viewpoints. Even with the increasing use of technology in determining and monitoring pregnancies, women approach this experience very differently. Technology has contributed to making pregnancy more of a visual experience. However, the effects of this visualization can differ considerably across cultures. Scholars like Squier (1996) have also argued that by making the experience of pregnancy a visual one, technology has constructed women as objects of medical gaze rather than as subjects defining their own experiences. Technology has contributed to the view that women are mere vessels for the fetus, and furthermore that the fetus and the woman are independent from each other, and in some cases, the view that the female body is a defective machine that cannot produce a healthy baby without medical intervention.

Women experience and respond differently to the use of technology, some "technologically" and others "organically" (Davis-Floyd, 1996). In the technocratic extreme, found in many American hospitals, the distinction between animate and inanimate is blurry (the insides of women can be examined in much the same way as the insides of a clock). Women who were influenced by this model tended to view their "selves" as their minds and not their bodies. Thus, the fetus was seen as a separate being, whose growth was only partially connected to the mother. Women who followed the organic model tended to view both body and mind as part of the self; thus, the mother and fetus were seen as growing together. These women were also more likely to emphasize the immediacy of their own experiences over the technological data (such as ultrasounds). There were also differences in what the two groups of women identified as "real." The technological view tended to emphasize the "thing seen," or the pictures on the ultrasound screen. From the organic worldview, the body of the woman itself was seen as the most real, the one "feeling" what was seen. The organic perspective was more of a personal worldview. The question then arises as to what kind of medical treatment or research is "ethical" from within such a worldview; do "ethics" impose particular imperialist perspectives when not placed under critique?

Mathematics

Mathematics has been defined by postcolonial scholars as a weapon of imperialism, as a covert method for spreading rationalism as a value. Western mathematics is based on the assumption that the world is composed of discrete objects that can be removed from their context (Bishop, 1995). In some African contexts, however, the personal and social world are seen as "knowable," but the world of objects is not, which contrasts with Western rationalism. The teaching of mathematics in schools, claims Bishop, was not just a neutral learning experience, but also part of the larger process of the imposition of rationalism's dehumanization and objectification on the world.

Western culture has tended to classify "nonliterate" cultures as simple or childlike based on the kinds of number concepts they use (although the concept of number is constructed and understood differently in diverse locations). Based on this concept, sweeping generalizations have been made about the lack of "logic" and "reasoning" to be found in non-Western cultures (Ascher & Ascher, 1997, p. 30). According to classical evolutionist mathematical scholars, the world is divided into prelogical and logical peoples. Prelogical people are considered to function in "mystical" rather than logical ways, a limitation that prevented them from recognizing obvious logical facts (like the use of the number five as a "natural" base for mathematical operations). The most common phrase to describe the logic of the prelogical was childlike, an epithet that persisted through many decades. As Powell and Frankenstein (1997) have commented, this distinction is not an innocent one. Putting forward the idea that some cultures are naturally deficient in mathematical knowledge has often led to situations where oppressed peoples participate in their own colonization by internalizing the views of the oppressors (Frieire, 1973). Further, the history of mathematics has in many ways been deliberately distorted; for example, the images in many early mathematics textbooks show Euclid as a "fair Greek" even though he lived and studied in Alexandria in Egypt and was a Black Egyptian (Joseph, 1997).

Mathematical concepts like Euclidean geometry have been reified as describing truths, rather than describing one particular way of viewing the world. Concepts like points, lines, and angles are essential to describe the world that the West has constructed. This thinking has influenced the ways in which mathematics has been created. However, as anthropological studies have shown (Carpenter, 1955; Neihardt, 1961; Urton, 1981), alternative constructions do exist and make powerful sense. Bloor's (1976) investigation of the history of mathematics found that alternative explanations for such mathematical facts as "one is a number" did exist but were relegated to what Martin (1997) calls the "rubbish bin of non-mathematics" (p. 158). Martin has also argued that the needs of contemporary capitalism have had a very strong influence in the development of the discipline of mathematics. The need to develop adequate methods for computation is, for example, tied to the development of computer chips. Another example is the influence of Western philosophies of individualism and a belief in competition on the development of such mathematical construct as game theory.

Mathematics does appear to be the intellectual embodiment of Enlightenment, modernity, and also Western colonialism. While we do not propose that mathematics be eliminated and do not believe that the suggestion would even be advisable, critique and the continued understanding that mathematics actually represents a limited form of thinking would be our recommendation. Much of what we have all come to depend on throughout the contemporary world is based on the field of mathematics. We would propose, however, that we develop dispositions though which we ask: What and whose knowledges are being silenced as we use mathematical theories? How are all of our ways of understanding and approaching the world being limited and narrowed?

FEMINIST DISCIPLINES: TROUBLING ACCEPTED KNOWLEDGES

Although there are multiple vantage points from which accepted knowledge is troubled and challenged (e.g., postmodernism, poststructuralism, queer theory, and certainly postcolonial theory, to name just a few), we would like to look more specifically at feminist perspectives, referring to them as feminist disciplines. Our intention is not to suggest that any of the problems or challenges have simple solutions. We do believe that feminist theories and research can provide important positions from which to conduct some types of postcolonial critique and to begin generating solutions. There are multiple feminisms that include content and ways of functioning that challenges dominant knowledges within the disciplines; placing feminist lenses on the disciplines reveals hidden knowledges and unthought-of possibilities.

One of the first possibilities raised by the notion of feminist disciplines is the issue of multiplicity. The common perception of an intellectual discipline includes the view of a certain wholeness, a speaking with one slightly changeable voice (as evidenced by the content of research, publications, and conference papers surrounding disciplines, often without the knowledge that "constructed" content in the field has already existed in other fields, all, however, consistent with and perpetuating the discourses of modernity). From a conventional, modernist perspective, multiplicity is even labeled a sign of deviance and inadequacy. Further, the accusation is made that women are just not fully rational enough to come up with a proper discipline of their own. Thus, right from the beginning, feminisms collided with the very idea of what a modernist intellectual discipline is and attempted to subvert and reconceptualize the notion.

An example of multiplicity within feminisms deals with notions of gender identity. Motherhood, wifehood, and sisterhood illustrate. Although motherhood may not be seen as an academic discipline, there is no disputing the fact that it is a social institution that has influenced the lives of probably all women (as even those who choose not to be mothers and are often criticized by society). Women are expected to be the sole caregivers for their young children, with only minimal support from outside the home, even in Western societies that appear to reject the children (Bulbeck, 1998; Greer, 1984). Much of early Western feminist writing rejected the concept of motherhood itself as imprisoning and limiting. Similarly, wifehood is problematic; research like that of Coltrane (1992) shows that in societies where women have more financial independence, men have more intimate relationships with their children and the women are less deferential to their spouses. Sisterhood is seen as coming from this dual rejection of wifehood and motherhood (Bulbeck, 1998). However, the term sisterhood is not without complications and contradictions. It suggests a bond between woman in equal social positions. For many women of color, this is not how they view their bonds with White women. Furthermore, within many African American communities, the word sister takes on other political meanings; sister implies that the women is neither an auntie (a White family's nursemaid) nor a woman of loose morals. However, when White women use the word sister in relation to Black women, an implication of shared experience may be made that Black women are not willing to accept. Feminisms and multiplicity imply complexity, diverse personal life experiences, and simultaneous, multiple ways of interpreting the world.

Another example that demonstrates the complex nature of the kinds of issues and content that feminism includes, as well as pointing toward the need for more postcolonial critique, is the whole question of population policies. The very term population policy means very different things to women of privilege than to women on the margins. For women of privilege, discourses about population often have to do with reproductive choices; whereas for many poor women (mostly those of color), population policies mean state agendas with which they are expected to comply. International organizations often refer to the need for third world countries to "control" their populations, which is seen as the reason for their poverty (not the centuries of direct and indirect exploitation that many of them have endured). During colonialism's heyday, women in colonized countries were encouraged to produce many children, to supply workers for the Empire. The reproductive activities of the poor have often been simply controlled (whether to reproduce or not) by those in power. Population policies have also responded to ideas like eugenics (selectively increasing certain parts of the population); in Nazi Germany, Aryan women were not allowed to use contraceptives and had to pay taxes if they did not have children within the first 5 years of their marriages (Bulbeck, 1998). Similarly, in Canada, according to Thobani (1992) there is concern that (White) Canada will be overrun by immigrants of color, so White Canadian women are increasingly encouraged to have children.

Population policies, which are so intimately linked to the lives of women and children, have also been (not surprisingly) linked to the discipline of economics. Bulbeck (1998) has shown how powerful American philanthropies, such as the Ford Foundation and the Rockefeller Foundation, supported schemes that focused heavily on family planning. However, the kind of methods used reflects a type of neocolonial agenda; the focus is on methods that are "women-proof," and that are efficient if not always completely safe.

One of feminism's major contributions is to work from the inside and to become a part of what is broadly called science, to offer feminist lenses to the range of disciplines generated by modernity. Feminist science studies are composed of a wide variety of approaches and perspectives, all of which share (to some extent) the conviction that a "focus on gender, race, class and sexuality and their intersections enriches our understanding of the emergence and use of scientific knowledge within and through social processes" (Wyer, 2001, p. 72). For example, the work of the Nobel Prize-winning developmental biologist Barbara McClintock looks at cells and "liberates DNA from its authoritarian past and puts it in a more responsive, more cooperative relationship with its cytoplasmic neighbors" (Henry, 2001, p. 87). Henry explains McClintock's theory as focusing on how DNA is impacted by its environment and how its genetic development itself is impacted by its surroundings. This focus on communication, interrelationships, and the impact of observers and observed on one another is cited by Henry as an example of the perspectives that have been lacking in traditional science and of how they can be enriched and transformed by feminist perspectives.

Thus, feminist science scholars challenge one of the foundational assumptions of science, namely, that science is neutral and objective. Feminist scientists have suggested that human knowledge is produced through "human action and intention," and that facts are "less a product of objectivity and experimental method than of social consensus about the adequacy of experimental evidence" (Henry, 2001, p. 73). Wyer (2001) has identified four broad themes that make up feminist science: (1) work that has looked at such critical issues as the history of women in science (Cabre, 2001; Rossiter, 1982; Schiebinger, 1989); (2) work that examines how scientific research has impacted women's lives, especially reproductive technologies (Clarke & Olesen, 1999; Gordon, 1990; Shiva, 1989); (3) work that focuses on how knowledge of the natural world has been distorted by the gendered and racialized nature of scientific methods and assumptions; and (4) work that looks at how science is taught in the classroom and the values that are transmitted as part of this process (Mayberry & Rose, 1999; Rosser, 1990). Feminist science studies have both a deconstructive and a reconstructive component in that the perspectives attempt to decipher how the absence of women as both research subjects and initiators of scientific inquiry has affected the construction of knowledge, while at the same time examining how scientific inquiry changes when new theories are constructed that do include those perspectives (Wyer, 2001). Feminisms offer challenges to and new ways of thinking about the disciplines that have dominated the Western colonialist intellect. We would suggest that diverse feminist voices offer much to postcolonial critique of realms of power and colonial influence.

3

METHODOLOGIES OF CONTEMPORARY COLONIZATION
Inscribing and Reinscribing Authority over "Others"

[T]he subaltern can, of course, speak, but only (allowed) through *us*, through our institutionally sanctioned authority and pretended objectivity ... which gives us the power to decide what counts as relevant and true.

—Beverly, 2001, p. 233

I will no longer be made to feel ashamed of existing. I will have my voice: Indian, Spanish, white. I will have my serpent's tongue—my woman's voice, my sexual voice, my poet's voice, I will overcome the tradition of silence.

—Anzaldua, 1987, p. 81

Imperialism continues to be associated with direct physical power. However, a range of so-called postmodern, as well as, postcolonial interpretations and critiques have demonstrated that hegemonic epistemological orientations, dominant languages, and privileged discourse practices generate power for particular groups of people over others. This power is constructed as intellectual, as an expectation for ways of being, as privileging particular emotions, and as disciplinary desires. We agree with academic theorists and cultural workers who suggest that (although we should never forget that violent physical colonization still exists in locations around the world) contemporary forms of Empire are much less direct, more seductive, and invoke the mask of progress by using notions of "cultural enlightenment and reform" (Gandhi, 1998, p. 14). This power does not necessarily require direct physical control. The power is netlike and is always everywhere (Foucault, 1980, p. 98), in the construction of colonizing discourses, institutional structures, and unquestioned technologies. Contemporary methods that are used to construct these less obvious, but no less dangerous, forms of Empire require revelation, critique, and resistance.

In this chapter, the way that colonizing power is both produced and reproductive of itself is discussed. Additionally, colonizing power places particular groups of people in the margins, signifying them as "others" who are less advanced in thinking, underdeveloped, unqualified to speak, and undeniably less human than those with power. These subaltern "others" (e.g., physically colonized, people of color, women, poor, children) are increasingly attempting to generate positions from which to resist, act, and to be heard. This chapter also addresses what happens when these subalterns speak—when the web of power is challenged.

CONSTRUCTING AND MAINTAINING COLONIALIST POWER

A number of scholars have discussed the conceptualization and creation of power. The most prolific and widely sited of these scholars is Michel Foucault, a poststructuralist, French philosopher/historian of the 20th century. Although Foucault did not directly discuss colonialism or Empire, he has provided perhaps the most in-depth overall conceptualization of power and the way it is both produced and produces (Olssen, 1999). Foucault explored methods of inclusion and exclusion by explaining technologies of power, systems of surveillance, and governmentality (Bhabha, 1994; Scott, 1995; Young, 2001). Postcolonial scholars have both used and critiqued Foucault's work in ways that provide unique insight into the complexities and workings of colonialist power, especially related to the social, emotional, and intellectual inscription of particular views of the world as dominant, even as superior. These views are interpreted as more advanced, scientific, rigorous, and embedded within superior value structures, while others are labeled as poor, confused, not developed, literally unreasoned, wretched, and lacking.

Power as Produced and Producing

Following a juridico-discursive model, power is traditionally explained as linear and unidirectional, possessed and employed from the highest points of a central source (e.g., the state, the economy, or the law), and used mainly to repress or control (Sawicki, 1991). Foucault, however, challenged traditional approaches by arguing that power: (1) is exercised rather than possessed by individuals, classes, or states; (2) arises from the bottom up rather than flowing from a centralized source; and (3) is productive as well as repressive. According to Foucault (1980), power is a web through which individuals are always circulating. We do not disagree with the traditional explanation as one interpretation, especially as related to physical aggression or capitalist domination. We do, however, agree with Foucault that power can be analyzed as more complex, as produced by human beings, while at the same time producing privilege for particular groups, naming (labeling and limiting) other particular groups, and reproducing itself. Power can be invisible, masked in discourses of freedom. As Foucault has illustrated, power can emanate from multiple locations, from unquestioned societal assumptions to marginalized positions of resistance.

Discourse as a Mechanism of Power. The idea of discourse is one that Foucault and other postcolonial scholars have dealt with in great detail as a concept and practice that is both ambiguous and fluid. The links between discourse and power, or more accurately, the ways in which discourse functions as a mechanism of power, have been extensively explored. Foucault explains discourses by stating that they include the language and practices that "systematically form the objects of which they speak" (Foucault, 1972, p. 49); although we want to avoid truth-oriented definitions, we can think of discourses as including events, things, and pieces of language that mirror socially constructed norms and ideologies. Example discourses include the enlightenment focus on reason; global conversations concerning human rights; a capitalist focus on free markets; the religious belief in a supreme being; constructs that ground fields or subfields of study such as human development; contemporary calls for accountability; and constructions of family as definable.

According to Foucault (1980), "it is in discourse that power and knowledge are joined together" (p. 100). Discourses are rooted in human ideas, institutions, and actions, making it difficult for individuals to think outside of them. Therefore, discourses become exercises in power and control, even though purposes underlying the discourses can range from liberation to oppression (Loomba, 1998; Viruru & Cannella, 1999). Foucault has argued that since the 19th century the dominant structures of Western society have reproduced themselves through such discourses. Human beings have internalized the systems, conformed to them, and submitted to their power. Further, discourse as a mechanism of power functions in the creation of systems of knowledge governed by rules of exclusion for what can and cannot be spoken, acted upon, thought, or tolerated.

Discourses are also described by Foucault (1980; 1982) as forms of power that shape, regulate, and normalize the people who are the discourse subjects (i.e., all of us who are in the discourse environment), subjects are invisibly and sometimes visibly created as normal/abnormal and as qualified/disqualified within the discourse. Discourses have played a crucial role in constructing and "normalizing" modern society, serving as vehicles through which populations have been organized, productivity defined, and order maintained.

Rules/Technologies of Power. Discourses, and the webs of power thus produced and producing within them, are governed by emergent *rules of formation* that create regulations for what is accepted and excluded (Foucault, 1972). These regulations are not concepts or themes, but systems of rules that govern the limits of the discourses determining such issues as: Who is given the right to speak? How is the authority created (e.g., qualifications, legal sanctions, forms of dissemination like publication, institutions)? How are concepts allowed to emerge? What are the restrictions on the content? What rules are applied to change or transform content? What are the rituals that determine ways of functioning within the discourse? How is contradiction handled?

Based on Foucault's interpretation of power, we all function within discourses, whether dominant discourses of capitalism and free markets that permeate the United States, or patriarchal, male-oriented discourses that are powerful around the world, or more marginalized discourses such as the celebration of diversity or indigenous ways of knowing. Discourse systems make technologies that discipline and regulate groups possible. These objectifying practices inscribe particular ways of functioning on human bodies. *Disciplinary power* is imposed on bodies by creating the *desire to be "normal"* (a normality created by the discourse). Individuals construct standards through which they judge themselves (Foucault, 1978). As examples, the desire to be a good girl, a good mother, or a good teacher (however these desires are defined) are all disciplinary technologies imposed on females in Euro-American society. The language of values, usefulness, productivity, accountability, and even empowerment are used to conceal disciplinary power. Individuals become more docile, judge themselves from within the discourse, and reproduce the power structure. These discourses are constructed within schools, hospitals, the media, and professional fields like psychology. Good teachers are reflective, professional, and follow accountability standards; good parents are sensitive, responsive, firm, and provide moral guidance, if responsive to disciplinary power.

Regulatory power, a technology that is less hidden but more difficult to challenge, constructs the "normal" though policies, laws, and legislated forms of intervention into people's lives. Examples of regulatory power in the United States include immunizations required for schooling, the recent inclusion of marriage as tied to social welfare benefits for the poor, and recent attempts to legislate that marriage can only be a heterosexual activity. Regulatory power, so often in the form of laws and policy, requires that everyone yield to the beliefs/perspective held by a particular group. The questions become: Who constructs the regulations? Whose voices are heard? Whose are excluded? Who is impacted and how?

Governmentality. As is implied through the explanation of regulatory technology, Foucault's notion of power is that it is embedded within the system of "order, appropriations, and exclusions by which subjectivities are constructed and social life formed" (Popkewitz & Brennan, 1999, p. 18). The creation of the modern Western world can be described as a process through which the "state," rather than the "prince," became the patriarch of the people. A governance of a different kind emerged as the phenomenon of "population" developed. Population was an entity that could be counted, measured, organized, labeled, and cared for by the state, yet the concept provides the illusion that governance ends, that the people are in charge. Governmentality became a kind of patriarchy of the people, by some of the people, for some of the people. As governmentality addresses population, both techniques of the self (e.g., individualization) and institutional technologies (e.g., totalization) become intertwined (Gordon, 1991).

Surveillance in Discipline and Punish. Foucault (1977) discusses the development of a technology of power that has been rarely questioned when employed against physically colonized or imprisoned people and has been accepted as common practice for researchers and adults who work with children. This technology is the practice of observation or surveillance. Initially, a panopticism was built in to the architecture of prisons to enhance visibility for guards over prisoners; the purpose was to control or neutralize "dandergous social elements" (Rouse, 1996). The architectural power was first initiated in isolation institutions like prisons, hospitals, schools, and factories. The techniques of surveillance were, however, gradually adapted and applied in a wider range of institutions and in various contexts, even to the point of becoming a philosophically accepted method for viewing others.

Surveillance creates an always, everywhere disciplinary technology. Using predetermined standards of "normality," observation and judgment of oneself and others is accepted. Hierarchical observation is constructed as supervised supervisors observe others; discipline is effective because everyone understands that they are being observed and may be punished. Surveillance has been manifested in the creation of examinations, whether scholastic tests or medical exams (Foucault, 1977). According to Foucault, practices of surveillance and documentation constrain behaviors by narrowing the range of what is considered appropriate, by creating practiced docile bodies.

Resistance and Freedom

The description of power to this point can easily be interpreted as a total, covert method for the construction of and control over others without always even needing the application of physical force, and we so absolutely want to remember this hidden web of control as a possibility. (See examples in Cannella, 2001; Demas, Cannella, & Rivas, 2003.) Further, Foucault's work is probably most often criticized for being a description of power that is so invasive that it appears to control us all. However, he does not actually construct people as without agency. First, most of the work is about systems, networks, and hierarchies—not about individuals. Yet, obviously the subject is implicated within notions of disciplinary/regulatory power, desire, and normality. Unmasking ways that power is exercised actually creates avenues for individual action, for example, functioning as a mother in the ways that one feels comfortable (not based on societal pressures to be the good mother), accepting one's sexuality and sexual orientation, creating spaces in one's field of work where knowledge that does not dominate is appreciated. Second, while Foucault's work focuses on the complexities and productive capabilities of power, he also addresses notions of resistance and freedom.

Where there is power, there is resistance (and also somewhat productive view). He states: "We're never trapped by power: it's always possible to modify its hold (Foucault, 1978, p. 13). He explains that power may only arise when resistance is present and that "power is exercised only over free subjects and only insofar as they are free" (Foucault, 1982, p. 221). According to Foucault, freedom refuses to submit to power, functioning as a kind of "permanent provocation" (p. 222). He further stresses that power relations and a freedom that permeates are inherent in all social contexts. For Foucault, geneological critique (analyzing the structures within a discourse and the network of power created within the structure, similar to postcolonial critique) is an avenue for the practice of freedom. Rajchman describes freedom for Foucault, "Freedom does not basically lie in discovering or being able to determine who we are, but in rebelling against those ways in which we are already defined, categorized and classified" (Rajchman, 1984, as cited in Sawicki, 1991, p. 27). His critiques created specific positions from which he chose to act. He constructed methods of participation for prisoners in the conceptualization of prison reform (Sawicki, 1991) and became involved with student activism in Tunisia in the 1960s (Young, 2001). He demonstrated that ethnology can be used on one's own Western culture, but that it is not appropriate for non-Western societies because it is embedded within structuralist science (Foucault, 1970). Foucault constructed resistance as rebelling against dominant definitions and categorizations in specific, purposeful ways.

Postcolonialism and the Campaign of Power

Gandhi (1998) has used Foucault's ideas about power to explain what she calls the "colonised's complicity in the colonial condition" and suggests that the campaign of power is frequently "seductive" (p. 14). In many colonial contexts, although power may manifest itself in a show of force, it is also equally likely to appear as "the disinterested purveyor of cultural enlightenment and reform" (p. 14), thus reproducing itself in ways that are less visible, but no less invasive and controlling. Related to the notion of resistance, but also to the reinscription of domination, power becomes the cycled response to situations in which it is exercised. The subjects of power collaborate in its dissemination in a variety of ways that range from direct resistance to speaking with and reinforcing the "master's" voice. The dominant values and structures of Western society reproduce themselves by working on and within the human subject, creating the desire to conform to what is expected within the society (Loomba, 1998).

Nandy (1993) also adapted Foucault's analysis of power to account for what Gandhi (1998) called the "particularly deleterious consequences of the colonial encounter" (p. 15). Colonialism is interpreted as having worn many masks, as changing style and strategy as needed. The first kind of colonialism, Nandy argues, is the more straightforward, aimed at the physical conquest of territory. The second is less direct and focuses on colonizing people's minds, selves, and cultures. This more insidious form is troubling because it was pioneered by so-called rationalists, who believed in advancing thought in backward lands, liberals who hoped to save the world, and modernists who believed they were bringing order and civilization to places that both lacked and needed enlightened civilization.

Said (1978) used Foucault's early explanations of discourse to demonstrate the way that "knowledge" about, and construction of, the orient reflected the power of colonial discourses. The writers and political thinkers who contributed to the construction of "orientalism" as an institution engaged in a form of violence that imposed a type of linguistic order on the world identified as oriental (Young, 2001). Western writings on the orient led to the institutionalization of systematic of ways of thinking about and seeing a particular part of the world that had no necessary relation to the cultures that actually existed. Discourses of the orient created an image of what countries and peoples in a particular geographic location were like and subsequently used those images to further colonize the "real" people of the region. Further, an archaeology of silence (Foucault terminology) was created in which knowledge about the orient excluded the voices of the "other" (those who actually lived in the region) from being heard.

Although postcolonial scholars have found Foucault's ideas about power insightful, the explanations have also been seen as highly problematic. Loomba (1998) explains that although seeing power as a "netlike" force that is already everywhere can be useful, the ways that institutions and regimes of truth join together to create the social fabric of power is unclear (p. 41). Said (1984) finds Foucault's concept of power that operates in a capillary fashion as disenabling to concrete forms of political criticism. Overall, postcolonial critiques appear to be concerned with power that is defined as appearing inescapable. Resistance and social change must be possible?

Additionally, Foucault's analysis of power does not, conceptually or in theory (and certainly nothing was written), fully recognize the colonial experience. Focusing on how power works in European modern societies, where physical punishment and torture are uncommon, systems of physical repression and subjugation are not addressed in Foucault's work. Further, in many colonized societies, group membership is the common form of identity rather than individuation. Therefore, power operated through classifying people into groups, and the groups were then seen as possessing distinctive psychologies and bodies (Loomba, 1998; Vaughan, 1993). When entire groups are constituted as the "other," power takes on different forms. Rather than constructing methods for disciplining or regulating individuals, entire groups of people are attacked through their cultures, ideas, and value systems (Sharpe, 1993; Tiffin & Lawson, 1994). Long before Foucault, historians in Africa discussed the ways in which customs and traditions were invented and used by colonizers to control the colonized. These technologies serve as apparatuses of power that inscribe and maintain group-imposed forms of power (Vaughan, 1991).

Spivak (1996, 1999) has proposed that even when one recognizes the ways in which discourse and power control the way we think, the notion still exists that one can somehow go outside these structures and recover the "voices" of the subaltern. This, she argues, is to underestimate the power of colonized structures that have completely rewritten intellectual and cultural systems of thought. If we consider the possibility that all discourse is colonizing, we must be open to unthought-of directions and possibilities in our attempts to listen; we must think of notions of understanding as power oriented and even colonializing; we must conceptualize diverse notions of human complexity, partnership, and our struggle to live together in ways that avoid colonialist power and continual attempts to decolonize.

MAINTAINING COLONIALIST POWER: TECHNOLOGIES FOR THE CONTINUATION OF EMPIRE

Some of the most compelling questions that have been raised by postcolonial critiques are whether the marginalized or subalterns (e.g., those living with colonial legacy, those with ignored life experiences, those assigned by dominant society to the fringes) can speak and what happens when they do. The very use of the concept of speaking may be further complicating this issue. Using the concept of voice, belonging as it does to a framework of thought that is alien to many marginalized groups and to a framework familiar to more dominant groups, may create situations that further disempower. However, proceeding from a position that recognizes this complexity and the problems with concepts such as speech and knowledge (as colonizer constructs), we continue to believe in the importance of examining powers that continue to silence (and discredit) the range of marginalized voices, technologies that are used to colonize actions, beliefs, access to resources, and individual daily lives of individuals. We begin by discussing three of these technologies of power—the construction of invisibility/silence, representation through the co-optation of identities, and a technology of simplification. Finally, we illustrate specific examples of marginalized people "coming to power" and the technologies used against them.

Technology of Invisibility/Silence

One characteristic of the work of the marginalized is invisibility. On a concrete level, knowledge and activities mostly characterized as women's work illustrate this invisibility, for example, properly cared-for bodies (including those of children), clean and inhabitable spaces, well-run households. All of these are characterized by an absence of dirt, clutter, and disorder rather than by a presence. The invisibility of such work makes it even more difficult to defend as a legitimate form of labor. Furthermore, the more successfully it creates an invisible scaffold for what is defined as "real work," the more invisible it becomes, becoming reified into a form of nature. Similarly in many colonial situations, natives were seen as part of nature and the spaces they inhabited characterized as undiscovered. In the current global economy, the work of the marginalized maintains its invisibility as it is conducted mostly in overseas countries, less obvious to what Harding (1998) calls Northern eyes.

Stephan (2001) has shown how the process of colonizing Latin America was in many ways a making of the existing invisible. Thus a major goal for the 19th century in parts of Latin America was to not only change the habits and customs of people but to change the language by standardizing the use of correct grammar. Stephan has also illustrated how the social behavior that lacked inhibitions at cockfights and carnivals came to be replaced with demands for the silence and constraint in theaters. Progress or colonization, whichever term one preferred, came to mean regulation:

> Language and body, flesh and spirit, individual and group, citizens and cities began to be stigmatized by police, teachers, physicians and scholars who sought to repress, corset, discipline or wash bodies, streets and languages to eliminate miasma, mud and "uncivilized deviations." (p. 317).

The key point was in many cases to neither eradicate disease or filth but to instill a new ethics controlled by commercial values. Human labor was not to be wasted on carnivals and cockfights and feasts but had to be channeled into more efficient directions.

Whether by enforcing absence or demanding invisible silent presence, the ways of knowing and being of marginalized groups have been denied the status of being knowledge. Denied the opportunity to be a part of the systems within which they were constrained to operate, knowledges have remained unspoken and unwritten, whispered and passed over. Further, from an empiricist point of view, such considerations are irrelevant. Those who support the ideal of a culturally neutral science, which would produce "one uniquely universally valid perfect reflection of nature's order" has had no place for the questions raised by those outside the center (Harding, 1998, p. 153). The questions that arise from those invisible frameworks have been considered to have no place in knowledge production. Harding also documents how this exclusion of other knowledges and voices is neither accidental nor occasional. The growth of so-called modern technologies in the West has been accompanied by a decline in other knowledge systems around the world.

Technologies of Co-optation through Representation

Some believe that, since many people who come from formerly colonized groups have now gained access to representation in democratic societies, power is now equal and equitable. People with colonized histories and other marginalized groups are now considered to have voice. However, there are inherent problems in assuming that elected representatives can fully and adequately ensure that the perspectives of a diverse group of people are made visible (Williams, 1998). The condition of marginality does not eliminate diversity. Further, the concept of representative government is based on the concept of trust, not only in the representative but also in the fairness of the system. Lacking the necessary dimension of trust, members of marginalized groups may find the concept of representation pointless. Although political representation may be seen from the dominant perspective as an act of speaking, from other points it may actually be seen and experienced as silencing. Another fundamental assumption in a "democratic" system of representation is the idea that this is a way in which conflicts can be resolved or mediated, so that they do not destroy society as a whole. Questions that do threaten to change society as a whole are often suppressed. People from marginalized groups, whose experiences can cause them to question what may appear to be common sense, continue to be the ones whose voices are suppressed. Suggestions from marginalized groups that justice consists not just of hearing different voices and providing them representation, but also responding to them are the kinds of points that are often classified as disruptive. Voices such as Gloria Anzaldua's are often supressed or ignored.

> At some point, on our way to a new consciousness, we will have to leave the opposite bank, the split between the two mortal combatants somehow healed so that we are on both shores at once and, at once, see through serpent and eagle eyes. Or perhaps we will decide to disengage from the dominant culture, write it off altogether as a lost cause, and cross the border into a wholly new and separate territory. Or we might go another route. The possibilities are numerous once we decide to act and not react. (Anzaldua, 1987, pp. 100–101)

Technology of Simplification

One of the most common distinctions made between Westerners and those identified by the West as "others" is the idea of an individual versus a community self. For example, while Western discourse focuses on the individual, so-called third world women are seen as members of communities, bound in complex networks of family and tradition. Although there is certainly a great deal of research that shows how notions of the individual self may not be applicable in non-Western contexts, and that many women, when they do define the concept of self, do so in very different ways, this combining of a very diverse range of experiences into one category of "community orientation" is not only disempowering, but also a reflection of what can happen when the marginalized speak (Bulbeck, 1998). This creation of a single category or orientation, especially one set up in binary opposition to that of the dominant, becomes a method of silencing different voices and denying complexity. Rather than allow for a range of different interpretations, the acceptance of an individual/community binary silences marginalized voices by constraining them to speak only within certain boundaries. The notion of community, with its concurrent implications of homogeneity and lack of internal conflict as well as the resilience to withstand such preventable ills like poverty or violence, is a very convenient myth for those who do not wish to understand (Potiki, 1991).

The use of the veil as clothing provides an illustration of the complexity of some and the oversimplification of others. The use of the veil by Arab women is often seen as a mark of tradition and even of male domination. Yet, Indian women have commented on the irony of how, during colonial times, "native" women were taught by Victorians how to cover their bodies as that was a sign of civilization. Currently, veiled women who cover their bodies, are seen in need of civilizing. Veiling is also not practiced by all Muslim women, and it ranges from a turban to a head-to-toe covering. The veil has also been seen as liberating women from fashions designed to please males (Jones, 1993), or as representing an erotic rather than a pornographic culture (Brooks, 1995). Veiling can also be seen as an expression of an urbanized lifestyle, as veiling is less common in villages, or even to disguise one's social status, as the veil can hide cheap clothes (Chapkis, 1994). In colonial Algeria, the veil became a way in which revolutionary women could disguise themselves. Islamic women who travel abroad use the veil as "a retort to Western feminism's devaluation of the wife-mother role" (as cited in Bulbeck, 1998; Nakata, 1995). The veil "does not carry a single unvarying message, even at the same moment" (p. 33). Neither do marginalized nor subaltern voices represent a simple understanding of the world that can be easily labeled and interpreted by others.

DOMINATION AND ATTEMPTS TO BE HEARD: EXAMPLE STORIES

These technologies of invisibility/silence, representation, and oversimplification are obvious from reactions to both individual and group attempts to be heard from the margin or from their attempts to enter or reconstruct the center. We illustrate these technologies of power as found in the individual case of Rigoberta Menchú and the societal reactions to women as gaining power and voice in the 1960s U.S. civil rights movement.

Rigoberta Menchú: Discrediting an Individual Subaltern

Rigoberta Menchú received the Nobel Peace Prize in 1992 for her international work to end military terrorism in Guatemala, her native country. Although not the basis for the Peace Prize, Menchú had also gained attention with the publication of her testimonial text, *I Rigoberta Menchú: An Indian Woman in Guatemala* (Menchú & Burgos-Debray, 1984). This attention had placed her testimonial in the center of the culture wars in the United States in the 1980s. Academics influenced by civil rights movements of the 1960s had created critical wings of their disciplines and begun to expand the curriculum. Menchú's testimonial served as a resource in this broadening of curriculum content. Through her work, privileged American students engaged in issues of poverty, lack of personal choice, and physical insecurity in ways that most had never experienced; their reactions were intense, some even calling for mobilization. In December 1998 however, the *New York Times* published a front-page article reporting that after almost 10 years of research, an American anthropologist, David Stoll, had demonstrated that Menchú's testimonial represented lies and distortions (Pratt, 2001). The voice of the marginalized was certainly coming under attack.

Much has been written on the legitimacy of both Menchú's work in particular and her testimonial as a research methodology (Lather, 2000; McLaren & Pinkney-Pastrana, 2000). We do not here attempt to address the multiple issues that have been raised. We will focus briefly on our question What happens when the marginalized (in this case Rigoberta Menchú) speak? by addressing the context in which Menchú's voices was both heard and denied.

We can provide a feel for the context by describing Stanford University (the location of David Stoll's graduate work) during the time that Menchú's work became prominent. Stanford had gained particular visibility during the United States "culture wars," the clash between children of the civil rights movements and Ronald Reagan's dogmatic political right. Mary Louise Pratt (2001) refers to Stanford's Hoover Institution of War, Revolution, and Peace as the "intellectual seat of the Reagan revolution" (p. 31). The departments and programs at Stanford have, however, tended to function with a much more liberal profile than the Hoover Institution. During the 1970s, the university conspicuously attempted to become more diverse and inclusive, actively recruiting African American, Chicano, and Native American students. As with many institutions, as faculty, students, and curriculum expanded and diversified, traditionalists reacted. At Stanford this reaction resulted in a yearlong Western culture course requirement that was not received positively by the student body. Two years of debate followed, a debate that was placed in the national media by William Bennett in his attempts to construct an ideological pulpit. Books like *The Autobiography of Frederick Douglass, The Wretched of the Earth*, and *I Rigoberta Menchú* were characterized as barbaric, as inferior to the great Western books written by European men. Because Menchú's testimonial commonly appeared in critical analysis courses, the work was from the beginning attacked by the emerging group of New Right "scholars" like Dinesh D'Souza (1991) in *Illiberal Education: The Politics of Race and Sex on Campus.*(1991)

Into this context entered David Stoll as a doctoral student in anthropology at Stanford. While conducting thesis research in 1989, Stoll believed that he had found reported versions of events that contradicted those that had been described by Menchú; he began actively seeking further contradictions and writing about them. In 1999, just after the front-page article appeared in the *New York Times* in December 1998 about his work, he published the book *Rigoberta Menchú and the Story of All Poor Guatemalans*—a dissemination strategy that should also be examined (Pratt, 2001). Stoll stated that he wished to oppose the new orthodoxy in the academy that always critiques Western forms of knowledge as tied to domination (although we would suggest that critique of one piece of scholarship does not require such an oppositional statement unless opposing Western critique is the actual agenda). He obviously believed that truth is the point and wanted the reader to believe in his attempts to reveal the truth about what he believes happened (and who was there) related to the events described by Menchú.

Stoll uses obvious colonialist methods. First, he tries to discredit Menchú and the subaltern voice in general by introducing diverse others who would have different stories and voices. He states that there are many different "legitimate Mayan" voices and that any of them could "make disleading generalizations about Mayas" (Stoll, 1999, p. 247). Further, Beverley(2001) points out that Stoll's method, appealing to heterogeneity by creating the terminology "any of those people," reinscribes power for the objective researcher/outsider (himself), and resignifies Menchú as "native," rather than one with authority to create her own form of representation (p. 234). His method uses the stereotyping of diversity to create individuals who cannot be heard and are consequently again invisible. Second, Stoll critiques Menchú as having a political agenda that is not appropriate for representing objective truth, while at the same time denying his own agenda to control who can be heard and to determine who has the authority to narrate. Finally, he states that Menchú assumes the authority that has been denied her and her people to speak "in the way she feels will be most effective" (Beverley, 2001, p. 233), without using a voice that necessarily follows some sort of empirical objective truth orientation. Menchú's voice does not allow Stoll's Western biases for how one should speak to maintain control. Stoll, therefore, attempts to counter the power created by Menchú when her voice is no longer subaltern (Beverley, 2001) as related to agency against elitist power (Guha, 1988). When the marginalized speak and appear to be leading reconstructions of center locations, when the marginalized are no longer invisible, many of those who have dominated the center move to maintain their power, to recolonize, discredit, and deligitimize.

U.S. Women and Power: Fear and the Reinscription of Misogyny

The voices gained by women in the United States during the 1960s so threatened some conservatives that a New Right emerged by the late 1970s. This group has demonstrated fear and hatred on at least two fronts: (1) The diverse voices of women (and anyone else who might represent difference) created a potential challenge to the patriarchal status quo; many felt threats to the power they did not wish to share. (2) The hatred, fear of, and contempt for women that is embedded within patriarchal Enlightenment revealed itself as women began to voice their experiences from the infinite positions from which they are located and attempted to claim equity and acceptance from those multiple positions. The collective hatred of women was no longer always masked by notions of patriarchal discourses of sexual difference or male protection. Those who were consumed by this fear and hatred set out to regain the nation—to reinscribe misogyny—using specific strategies that would lead to particular narrowed public discourses and institutional changes that would tightly control the web of power, rather than expand networks of possibility across diverse groups of people and perspectives. These narrowed public discourses and institutional changes are, of course, intertwined. For clarity, however, we will attempt to illustrate them separately, while at the same time demonstrate how the strategies produce and reinscribe each other.

Discourses That Demonize: When Women Choose Not to Be "Good Girls."
In the spring of 2001, a cartoon appeared in our local Bryan/College Station, *Texas Eagle* newspaper that showed a woman dropping her child at a "daycare" center, as the "female" child begs to go home. While the mother responds "No honey, I want my career, our house, and my new car," the "obviously" "impotent" now silenced and invisible father stands behind the mother and says nothing. In the meantime, the environment of the daycare center is represented by scary pictures, monster teachers, and children who are running all over the room with the evil on their faces that clearly displays the early experiences of future serial killers (our interpretation of the artist's message). In one cartoon, the artist has demonstrated the multitude of discourses that have either been constructed or reconstructed over the past 30 years to silence, discredit, and further marginalize women. Beginning with the narrow reinscription of woman as heterosexual, mother, and hearth angel martyr, those who identify themselves as female are again blamed for the creation of evil children, impotent males, and, in general, all the problems in a society. Further, in this cartoon those who would challenge "female" or "male" identified normality are "set up" to be labeled as antifamily, selfish and uncaring, and without moral values.

We know that these discourses are not new. Women in the United States (and many other societies) have historically been treated with disrespect and contempt, they have found themselves continually reinscribed as marginal. Authors like Faludi (1991) have demonstrated this in everything from trends in antifeminism, to the construction of unwed witches, to the New Right's politics of resentment. We would propose, however, that over the past 30 years, the discourses have taken on a new power, perhaps less visible but consequently more dangerous; this power amounts to an unquestioned acceptance by some who have previously considered themselves supportive of equal rights and entirely open to diversity. Discourses of moral decay, family/middle-class values, and antifeminism have been used to create, not simply a backlash, but a massive social movement. The purpose of this backlash is to counter the movement in which women have begun to be heard from the diverse sites from which they live and construct the world, have begun feeling more comfortable as part of the dialogue, and have begun to influence the political climate in the United States and around the world. As women's anger over patriarchal injustice and issues like equal, gay, and reproductive rights gained voice, the fear of difference emerged, especially as this large group of people who had traditionally been marginalized politically was being heard and seen as gaining power. Contemporary misogynous discourses were generated from past patriarchy and inscribed with new powers through reconstructed American institutions (like family, morality, and most recently, patriotism) as discourses that were no longer open to criticism.

This reinscription was influenced in its inception by a variety of groups that include: people who for numerous reasons fear change and especially loss of power; those (like women) who have learned well to perpetuate the oppression and disqualification of members of their own groups; people who have used scholarly or religious "truth" to ground their identities and are unconsciously threatened when their life truths are questioned; and even those who are concerned about equity, oppression, and voice, yet because of the complexities of their own material, daily survival accept the discourses. We know that the founding of such groups as the Eagle Forum, Concerned Women for America, and the Moral Majority (Berry, 1997) represent some of the more public beginnings of the massive contemporary movement against women and other marginalized voices against sexism and patriarchy. However, we believe that the systematic power to silence, reconstruct as invisible, and remarginalize has been underestimated. Would we call the movement to resilence women a "vast right-wing conspiracy" against the voices of the marginalized, or a well-organized, longitudinal agenda that would regulate large groups of people in a democracy in which (after all) majority rules? Actually, either description would work and we believe that either is disturbing. Both point to the recognition that when women began to be heard from their multiple marginal positions, organized systems for silencing and reconstructing positions of invisibility emerged (positions of power and oppression). Some of these systems have been purposely planned, organized, and implemented; others have emerged accidentally.

The reimposition of a family values discourse on women is one example. Using the historical construction of power over women in the name of child welfare (Cannella, 2001), the New Right moved to silence the emerging discussion of discrimination, equity, and social justice with discourses like family values and morality that would reproduce patriarchy. Since we all value the people who are close to us (e.g., family, friends), signifiers, like family, were asked to critique yet from within such narrow boundaries that attempts to broaden (e.g., including diverse family structures) were disqualified and labeled as lacking. These signifiers were imposed on a variety of groups, under a range of conditions, and from a cultural perspective that judged those who did not "fit" the definition.

A series of interrelated public policy discourses were created. Editorials, books, public announcements, conservative language from newly formed NGOs of all types attacked the Equal Rights Amendment, gay rights, and women's rights over their own bodies. These attacks claimed that a decline of family and societal values was caused by such notions as sexual freedom and equal rights, labeling women who believed in liberation as male-haters (hooks, 2000). Conservatives took advantage of what some would call historical amnesia regarding the 1950s' family, and what others might call ignorance, to create a "fictional" family that engaged in a heterosexual wedded bliss that was supported by patriarchal submission legitimized as necessary because of differences in the sexes (Coontz, 1997). Conservatives legitimated this reinscription of patriarchal sexism by blaming a variety of societal circumstances and the people in them including poverty (especially poor women) and the newly emerging voices of women in the academy. These examples briefly illustrate the 30-year construction of discourses that have demonized the voices of women as they have attempted to speak from the margin.

The presidency of Ronald Reagan resulted in an environment in which women, especially poor women, could be constructed as the group that should be held responsible for economic conditions in the country. Reagan assaulted the welfare of poor citizens because he disliked the notion that individuals could at times in their lives need assistance and because he followed a fiscal model that assaulted the economic well-being of the state itself as well as supporting institutionalized systems of inequity. When this fiscal model resulted in unbelievable federal deficits, poor women became the scapegoats. Using the work of individuals like Anderson (*Welfare: The Political Economy of Welfare Reform in the United States*, 1978) and Glider (*Wealth and Poverty*, 1981), language and actions emerged that blamed societal economic problems on the growing number of poor mothers who were labeled as immoral and lazy (Trattner, 1999; Weaver, 2000). Poor women (and by implication all women) were blamed for having children without resources, while both the need for equalizing mechanisms for labor and care and the sexist messages that would have women provide hearth and home for the good of their children were ignored. By 1996 a discourse of welfare reform had been constructed that labeled women as immoral, not married, lazy, incompetent, and lacking responsibility (the Welfare Queens). Welfare reform was legislated that required the growing poor, who were increasingly single-parent women, to work longer hours, limit themselves to a small amount of public assistance, and to be *married* (Cannella, 2001; Haskins, Sawhill, & Weaver, 2001; Marshall, 2001; Rector, 2000). The requirement for marriage was not publicized; it was simply and quietly passed (without critique) as part of the reform effort that would later be used to construct a pro-marriage dialogue and even further legislation in the 2002 reauthorization effort. As 2002 approached, newspaper articles, legislative testimony, presidential documents, and legislation passed by the House of Representatives (just to name a few) supported an agenda that would reappropriate funds to provide assistance (for such activities as the recovery of child-support moneys) over programs that would teach marriage in high school, give money to states for marriage incentives, and create privilege for those in heterosexual marriages (Cannella, Demas, & Rivas, 2002). Certainly this 30-year organized discourse has reimposed, however invisibility, a patriarchal reinterpretation on poor women and begun the process of using poor women and their children to further silence all women.

Even women who would be considered privileged have not been immune from this organized reaction to their attempts to be heard. This reaction to the voices of the marginalized has been illustrated in the construction of both antifeminism and monointellectualism in the academy (Lincoln & Cannella, 2002). Scholars, especially female feminist scholars, who construct forms of research, publication, and teaching that do not follow the linear, progressive assumptions of truth-oriented science have been accused of creating a "victims revolution" (D'Souza, 1991) and of betraying other women (Sommers, 1994). Research topics have been dismissed as invalid and irrational (Ginsberg & Lennox, 1996). Some fields have even managed to either maintain or reinscribe the will to truth, linearity, and subjectivity using languages of standards and quality. Although publicly supporting the illusion that diverse scholarship is respected, competition and notions of rigorous science are used to reward individuals and legitimate capitalist orientations toward fund raising in the academy. Have you noticed, money and positivism are the top priorities? Scholars who bring in diverse ideas and methods are being accused of denying students the lessons of truth (Damon, 2000). Because of their openness to a variety of ideologies, humanities and social sciences are being labeled as threats to American freedom, safety, and prosperity (Balch, 2001).

Institutional Change. Finally, a reaction to the voices of women (and other marginalized groups in the United States) has come in the form of organized attempts to change institutions like the media, the judiciary, and academia. Special interest groups have joined with the business lobby and the Republican Party to create an environment that would legitimate particular forms of reasoning (stereotypic male linearity and competition) and discredit and marginalize others. Think tanks, foundations, and institutes have been constructed to train more conservative professionals, provide jobs and access to the creation of public discourse by those professionals, and to provide support for scholarship that advances dominant agendas (Cannella et al., 2002; Covington, 1998, Demas et al., 2003; Lincoln & Cannella, 2002). Newly created institutions have educated a group of people who cannot hear the voices of others, and further believe that these voices are un-American, dangerous, not moral, not reasonable, and are basically without legitimacy. Existing institutions now find themselves dominated by this new group of professionals and the resources that have constructed them. The diverse marginal voices of women (the voices that do not yield to patriarchy), perhaps more than any other group, are increasingly silenced.

CAN WE COUNTER REINSCRIPTIONS OF POWER?

This entire chapter has dealt with methods of colonization, whether the construction of webs of power or the reinscription of patriarchy, when those who have been marginalized or colonized begin to speak and be heard. We understand that the information can be disempowering and definitely depressing, yet, we do believe that the information must be disseminated. As Foucault has expressed, only where there is freedom is there power (even when the purpose of the exercise of power is to directly decrease freedom); further, power and resistance cannot be separated—were there is power, there is resistance. We actually believe that to counter the production and exercise of power that is oppressive we must know about the diverse experiences and perspectives of others. We must know about the different ways that power is explained, not because these explanations are truths but because they provide us with possibilities for escaping dominant Western philosophical and intellectual orientations that tend toward the colonizing of others. (Sometimes escape originates even from within those orientations, as with the critical perspectives invisioned by Foucault.)

Within the first three chapters of this book, we have both discussed and employed postcolonial critique and explained the possibilities generated by multiple feminist disciplinary perspectives and the critical postmodern views offered by Foucault for the analyses of networks of power. The methodologies themselves counter the reinscription of colonialist power, but, perhaps more important, the assumptions, constructions, and knowledge that are revealed using the methods result in locations from which specific actions may be generated. These actions can range from traditional radical activism that involves "taking to the streets" to standing up for knowledges and people who have been perpetually placed in the margins, to, in a variety of ways (whether in one's resident community, professional field, or daily life), challenging the limitations of Western perspectives that may be hurting people in the real world, to joining global organizations that would fight colonialism (whether intellectual, environmental, or economic), to generating ideas from the range of possible decolonialist activist activities that are as yet unthought.

In the next section of the book, the work is more specific as we focus on childhood and education. We begin by placing a postcolonial perspective on the construction of "child," a very Western, modern concept. We believe that children have been colonized as we have created them as psychological beings whose world we (as adults) can define, explain, and know. Further, contemporary discourses "use" them as objects of politics and global capitalism, as they (like "orientals") are created as the "other" who must be tested and educated. We believe that our postcolonial critique of the child and education is a beginning for multiple actions that would counter colonialist power.

Part II
Postcolonial Critique, Childhood, and Education

4
CHILDHOOD AND COLONIZATION
Constructing Objects of Empire

Childhood is the most intensively governed sector of personal existence ... linked in thought and practice to the destiny of the nation.

—Rose, 1990, p. 121

EXPLORING CHILDHOOD AS COLONIZING CONSTRUCT

As we have expressed both at the beginning of this book and in previous work (Viruru & Cannella, 2001a; 2001b), we believe that the construction of the child and the subsequent treatment of those who are younger in years should be considered through the lens of postcolonial critique. For a variety of reasons the labels, forms of representation, and positions imposed on those who are younger can be categorized as oppressive, controlling, and even colonizing. The consideration of these possibilities is one of the major purposes of this book.

However, we do not wish to perpetuate an "image of the angel caught in the storm" of colonialism (Burman, 1998, p. 60), of the innocent lacking any form of power. The multiple ways that younger human beings influence the world will never be understood and are certainly infinite. Further, we all live in historical moments that would appear to limit us, yet human beings (including those who are younger) surprisingly challenge the boundaries of time and history, of space and moment. Resistance, agency, and possibility are certainly notions that can be associated with those who are younger as well as those who are older. Actually, we believe that examining constructions, discourses, and institutions of the child and childhood as forms of colonization could serve to increase life possibilities. Postcolonial critique requires that adults place themselves in positions in which they must examine authority, power, knowledge, and even the will to understand. Adults must be willing to rethink and reconceptualize what they think they know about the child and childhood.

Although we want to purposely avoid the construction of a set of consistently tied, or even "correctly interpreted" theories, the work of postcolonial scholars can be used to explain reasons for the consideration of child as colonizing construct. First, and most easily related to the child, Bhabha (1996) discusses the production of the "other" (p. 37) though a colonial discourse generated by creating knowledge about the "other" through surveillance. The colonizing discourse creates a "subject people" (p. 37), who are described as lacking and in need of control by those who have generated the knowledge. Stated simplistically (although Bhabha has been critiqued for this simple decentering), oppression is legitimated over subject peoples based on the knowledge gained or constructed by observing them. Certainly the knowledge constructed by adults as they have chosen to place children under surveillance has been used to legitimate administrative systems of control over them (Viruru & Cannella, 2001a).

Said's initiation of postcolonial studies through the book *Orientalism* (1978) provides a lens through which childhood can be examined as colonizing construct. Said used Foucauldian conceptualizations of discourse and power to illustrate the ways in which colonizing European discourses created orientalism as a phenomena. Texts, constructed by European orientalists, used Western forms of representation—traditions, codes of understanding, signification, and perspectives on the world— to create an orientalist ideology consistent with European imperialism. While different locations labeled as the orient physically existed, beliefs about this "orient" were European inventions, visions that imposed constructions of the "other" as exotic and romantic. In this same sense, literature on the child has proliferated, using Western, Euro-American, and scientific visions (to be discussed more in the next section of this chapter). Just as physically there are countries labeled as the orient, those who are younger do physically exist and are smaller than those who are older. However, this existence does not prove or legitimate adult discourses. Further, those who have been labeled as children have been consistently seen as the same as the colonized, exotic beings who were different from adults and interesting only to the extent that they could be analyzed for who they would become (Cannella, 1997; Gandhi, 1998; Viruru & Cannella, 2001a).

Previously we discussed postcolonial scholars who have critiqued problems with focusing on discourse and power as if easily decolonized, as if colonialism were over and no remnants remained. Spivak (1996) has cautioned against the belief that one can function outside discourse structures that are in power. The voice of the other—the voice of children—may for a variety of reasons (e.g., survival, experience) be profoundly reflective of dominant colonizing discourses and the resulting power relations.

Additionally, JanMohamed (1985) and Parry (1987) have focused on the continuation of directly colonizing physical power. This physical power is reconstituted through institutions of colonialist control. Examples include the classification of people as the mild Hindu or the slow Black to stereotype and assign people to particular kinds of jobs and to limit life opportunities (Loomba, 1998). Those who are younger have certainly been categorized as in opposition to those who are older, as children versus adults. Often these younger human beings have themselves accepted the distinction and all the limits accorded. Further, they have been placed into the societal institutions that classify them as slow, gifted, or hyperactive, as well as innocent, incompetent, and savage, just to name a few of the institutionalized constructions that mentally and physically control.

These perspectives represent abbreviated reasons why we believe that it is important to place the construct of the child under postcolonial critique, why we suggest that childhood is a form of colonization that attempts to construct subjects, and even objects, of/for the Empire. To expand and provide depth to the critique, we first review the growing body of literature that has illustrated the Enlightenment/modernist bias underlying the construction of and beliefs about childhood. Additionally, the construction of science as objectifying truth for the Empire is examined.

REINSCRIBING WESTERN COLONIALIST IDEOLOGY ON THOSE WHO ARE YOUNGER

As mentioned in previous chapters, one of the most influential eras of European history was the Enlightenment. The belief systems that emerged from the 17th and 18th century Age of Reason are credited with introducing medical and environmental progress, scientific advances in transportation, construction, and communication, and even notions of democracy, equity, and justice, as well as modernism, capitalism, and socialism. Scholars who have examined the social construction of the concept of the child generally place this construction within Western Enlightenment and the further development of the concept within the more contemporary modern period. Therefore, Enlightenment/modernist perspectives cannot be ignored as we summarize the ways in which the concept of child has emerged. However, one aspect of European history that is almost consistently ignored in discussions of the child is the direct physical colonization and imperialist acts that were practiced by those same developers of so-called Enlightened and modern systems of thought. During this time period, both imperialism and colonialism were supported by the Enlightened focus on human progress. For example, technological improvements in ocean-going vessels made travel possible (as mentioned in chapter 2) and the subsequent control of others around the world (Young, 2001). As we provide an overview of the construction of the child concept, we infuse colonizing events that support the self-proclaimed Enlightened belief structure of the West that has proclaimed as both objects and subjects of Empire women, children, people of color, and those who would live in far-away lands.

By the 16th century, Europeans found themselves in turmoil, philosophically and religiously. Some had accepted Greek or Roman understandings of the world. Yet, a Christianity that interpreted Greek and Roman philosophy as pagan was gaining converts and strength. Conflicts were dealt with in a variety of ways that included revising Greek manuscripts written by scholars like Aristotle to be consistent with Christian theology, the construction of diverse sects of Christianity, and even religious wars. The most long-lasting reaction to the concern that the European community shared no common thought was, however, the increasing acceptance of the idea that natural laws or rules of nature existed that could be used to mediate relations between groups holding diverse beliefs and perspectives. The gaining acceptance of the concept of natural law was manifested in the belief that universal truths could be found in nature if only the correct methods were used. The way was paved for the construction of and belief in science as truth (Macpherson, 1962).

Discourses that both generated and reinforced this belief emerged. Philosophers like Bacon (England), Descartes (France), and Galileo (Italy) were accepted as authorities. For example, Descartes proposed that the world existed in two domains—the internal individual mind and the objective, truth-oriented world of nature. The use of this Cartesian dualism resulted in language, ways of viewing the world, and daily actions that inscribed as universal such perspectives as truth versus nontruth, mind versus matter/body, and objectivity versus subjectivity

(Lavine, 1984; Lowe, 1982). The various discourses of Enlightenment supported one another toward the belief that man (European middle- and upper-class man) was progressing in the discovery of predetermined human truths, advancing beyond human beings of previous times or contexts. According to Bacon, for example, the Greeks and Romans were simply children of civilization as compared to men of the Enlightenment (Bury, 1932), expressing the belief in superiority over both other cultures and those who are younger. Further, scientific thought (previously considered a passive activity) emerged as the generator of truth and understanding, as the eventual savior of the world.

The modern period of industrialization during the 19th and 20th centuries evidenced even stronger beliefs in progress and science, as knowledge has been viewed as accelerated while human beings have been described as moving toward forms of civilization that are increasingly more advanced. A positive faith in scientific reason has emerged that focuses on empiricism, objectivity, universals, and progress. This scientific reason was not simply applied to the physical but was assumed to also have the potential for uncovering and explaining human truths. From within this Enlightenment/modernist context, the "child" has been and continues to be constructed.

Creators of progressive, scientific, reasoned thought were not simply generating ideas; these Western perspectives were being taken around the globe through imperialist and colonialist actions. In some cases, the purposes were to extract riches, impose religion (usually Christianity), or to assert an imperialistic power over indigenous populations; in other cases, the purposes were less direct like settlement and trade (Burkholder & Johnson, 1998; Young, 2001). (See chapter 1 for further information.) Whatever the original purpose, the populations of mostly indigenous peoples of color became part of the discourse of progress that privileged White European male adults and placed those who were younger (labeled children) and colonized peoples in much the same positions—called savage, incompetent, out of control, and incomplete. This Western colonialist ideology continues to be accepted in contemporary rhetoric regarding children. They are described in ways that both embody and reconstitute Enlightenment/modernist views of the world.

While a number of scholars have written concerning views of those who are younger during various historical time periods (French, 1991; Jung & Kerenyi, 1963; Kennedy, 1988; Nicholas, 1991), most have agreed with Aries (1962) that the construction of child as separate from adult is grounded in so-called Western thought. As the creation of a belief in childhood is examined, dominant ways of interpreting and addressing the world, such as dualism, progress, and reason, emerge. Children have been created from within these specific forms of interpretation, are controlled and limited by them, and have become the objects whose existance reconstitutes them.

Dualism

The separation of child from adult was consistent with Cartesian thought (as mentioned previously) that distinguished mind from matter as an actual representation of physical material difference (e.g., small/large) and the representation of difference created through mind (e.g., innocent/knowledgeable, dependent/independent, savage/civilized). Further, the dualistic discourse was supported by (1) the belief in the Christian church that particular privileged males should be protected from the corruption of society as well as controlled themselves, and (2) the growing notion that White males who were older represented the most advanced form of human functioning. Binary thinking abounded and was physically enacted through newly emerging institutionalized ideas: good/evil, superior/inferior, right/wrong, adult/child, civilized/savage.

The dichotomous labeling and assumed accuracy of separation creates a privileged position from which adults function. For example, the assumption of childhood innocence implied ignorance as compared to the knowledgeable adult. Walkerdine (1984) has explained how this privilege has been used to both label children as deficient (as incomplete) and withhold knowledge in the name of protection. The knowledge that is part of the lives of younger human beings has been judged as either nonexistent or of poor quality; children are then labeled as a group for which surveillance, limitation, and regulation is necessary for their own good.

Silin (1995) provides a profound example of problems with the creation of an adult/child dichotomy in his discussion of illness and death. The innocence/intelligence dichotomy is shattered when someone faces suffering, loss, or separation. Adult knowledge and childhood innocence are called to question by the very circumstances of life when those who are younger appear to deal with death and illness in more knowledgeable ways.

Burman (1994) explains how the construction of child has been used to perpetuate a colonialist form of power. In the name of serving third world children, peoples of the first world are asked to make charitable donations; this charity would guarantee a childhood for poor children. This philanthropic stance masks the first world imperialism that has actually led to the poverty in the first place, constructs the illusion that third world people (or their "corrupt governments") have created their own physical life conditions, and represents the first world as the savior of all human beings (especially innocent children).

Further, focusing on a group identified as child (as if asocial, apolitical, and ahistorical) masks issues of gender, class, and culture as well as denies the knowledge of particular groups collaboratively generated by both the younger and older members of those group. The adult/child dichotomy perpetuates colonialist power by masking circumstances, creating societal conditions faced by all members of the group. Entire peoples are created as lacking—labeled as needy (the children) and corrupt, lazy, or underdeveloped (the adults).

Progress

The Enlightenment belief in progress has been so inscribed in the Western human psyche that it is assumed even in our daily conversations, especially regarding those who are younger. "He's learning more every day." "She is so smart, she'll be using logical thinking before long." We even label individuals as slow or abnormal when movement toward a particular direction of thought or physical ability has not occurred.

Yet historically we are reminded that the concept of progress is a fairly new human construction. For example, even in what has been identified as the West, the ancient Greeks were concerned with social order, not progress. The Greeks believed that human beings had already become resourceful enough and that the status quo should be maintained to avoid human degeneration (Bury, 1932).

Rejecting the "dark ghosts of the Middle Ages" (Cannella, 1997, p. 48) and embracing the emerging Enlightenment faith in science, scholars like Jean Bodin and Francis Bacon, however, proposed the notion of progress. New discoveries concerning the truths of nature were believed to represent scientific progress. This notion that both scientific knowledge and "mankind" were destined to advance emerged as an unquestioned belief. By the 1700s, this view of progress was also applied to human intellect, to describe particular groups as more advanced than others, and to describe changes that occur in individuals lives.

The acceptance of universal progress as a given and the search for universal laws to explain it directly influenced the construction of the belief in "child," while at the same time legitimating colonialism. For example, the most intelligent children in London or Paris were considered more advanced than the most intelligent children in Constantinople because of the progress make by Western European civilization. Herbert Spencer even expressed the belief (which was accepted by many) that the work of individuals, such as Newton and Shakespeare in the West, compared to the world created by "houseless savages" in the colonial world proved the advanced status of particular groups (Bury, 1932, p. 337).

Further, the search for universal laws generated claims that there were sequenced stages of change for animals that introduced the concept of development as an individual manifestation of progress. Although theories concerning the notion of development, especially as applied to human beings, have changed over the years, the construct has been taken up and accepted as truth (Morss, 1990). As Darwin (1979) (original work Darwin, 1859) stated, "all corporeal and mental endowments will tend to progress toward perfection" (p. 223).

Progress and the belief in development emerged as linear constructs that were not questioned and were most often interpreted in relation to Western beliefs in science and the privileging of European male constructions of reason. Challenges to this belief in linear advancement and improvement were ignored, even though contradictions ranged from the behavior of individual human beings, to knowledge that was treated as nonexistent, to diverse cultural ways of functioning, to the continued existence of violence and war. Moving forward was most often defined from within a scientific gaze that assumed predetermined hierarchical laws of nature that would apply to all beings (Mazrui, 1996).

From within this context, the belief in individual human development emerged—a belief that has been foundational to the construct of child. Important is the recognition that Enlightenment scholars were profoundly intrigued by the belief in their own superiority, the assumption that the understandings of the world generated by adult male Europeans were unsurpassed. Therefore, these emerging theorists (as the notion of theory was also constructed as part of Enlightened discourse) wanted to understand the development of their own thought, the forms of thinking that they considered the most advanced. Consistent with the newly emerging belief in objective surveillance, younger human beings were viewed as those who could be observed for information concerning the advanced adult mind. Children's minds were believed to prefigure, to foreshadow, the adult (male) mind because they represented a lower evolutionary state of "man"—a position also accorded those who were identified as primitive (usually, colonized people of color). If objective and Enlightened study could be conducted with children, the origin of man could be revealed. Children, beginning with infants, were seen as the evolutionary baseline for revealing human truths. Child study and later developmental psychology were created as the avenues for observation/surveillance, measurement/judgment that would reveal this human progress (Burman, 1994).

Voneche (1987) illustrates the actual lack of interest in the knowledge and abilities of those who are younger (unless tied to adult knowledge) in "The Difficulty of Being a Child in French-Speaking Countries." "When Victor (the wild child) came out of the woods, everyone knew what to do with him" (p. 62), teach him what is appropriate for human beings, not how to survive with animals. "Nobody cared to know more about his life in the woods of Aveyron. No one went along with him" (p. 63).

The belief in progress and its manifestations through human development emerged and were accepted as natural and unchangeable truths. The belief in development as described through stages has a variety of origins, not always even related to the concept of progress or change. As examples, the Greeks believed in the number 7—not in progress—so they used the number 7 to divide life into increments of 7 (Cannella, 1997). Espousing conventional patriarchy, the writng of prolific Enlightenment scholars like Rousseau supported notions of advancing hierarchy (Taylor-Allen, 1982); he even described stages like middle childhood as part of natural growth and development for inferior, prelogical, and irrational cultures as they progressed toward European adult forms of thought (Aries, 1962). Countless numbers of developmental scholars have created theories that are framed by the progressive stage construct. Piaget's stages of cognitive development illustrate both this unquestioned tendency toward assessing and describing human change as progress and the arbitrariness of concepts of development; for example, the time spent by younger human beings with family and in schooling during Piaget's early life corresponds to the age ranges that he "discovered" as developmental stages (Lichtman, 1987).

The assumptions of progress that have placed younger human beings at lower hierarchical levels than those who are labeled adult reinforces Enlightenment/modernist beliefs in the superiority of Western constructions of truth, science, and ways of interpreting the world. This position creates an environment of injustice and the legitimation of control over those labeled as children and also over groups of adults who do not fit or agree with the position. To explain this further, we want to demonstrate how the belief in human (child) development progress allows the privileged to subjugate the "other," fosters cultural imperialism, maintains hierarchical relations, and interprets human beings as deficient.

First, belief in progressive human development authorizes the placement of human beings into hierarchies, positioning people on a continuum between those who are the most advanced, developed, mature, and knowledgeable and those who are immature, innocent, and less logical. Individuals and groups who accept this continuum and function with the forms of knowledge that are inscribed as advanced are placed in positions of privilege; those who practice adult Western logic are placed in positions of power—over children and over cultures or societal groups who would choose other forms of knowledge and being. We commonly hear something like: third world peoples have not developed as far as we in the United States. Give them more time to overcome their corruption and poverty, and they will understand markets and technology like we do.

Second, although child development is labeled as a kinder, more humane, and just way of treating children, the notion is used to legitimate the regulation of one group by another. Whether human beings are labeled children, the poor, or underdeveloped peoples, the expectation that everyone passes through particular stages creates power for those who are at the so-called advanced levels of those stages. People who possess Western developmental knowledge are placed in positions to guide (read: regulate) others. A physical and intellectual imperialism is imposed as those who disagree and resist the power; the resisters are labeled uncooperative, ignorant, and needing intervention.

Third, developmental progress constructs a position in which someone (whether children, females, people of color, or adults identified as primitive) is always judged to be lower—inferior—less worthy—at the bottom. Women are good examples of those labeled (historically and in many societies) as less advanced; even perspectives that would increase opportunities for females judged as less advanced than those who have not been allowed to develop independence because of societal experiences (Walkerdine, 1988, 1989). Independence is not even examined as a male-oriented construct embedded in dominant discourses of "advanced human functioning."

Finally, with the possible exception of those who have reached the highest levels of development, human beings are viewed as incomplete. The focus on always becoming more advanced establishes an environment in which many of us will never be satisfied. Children have been labeled as the human beings whose life purpose must be to overcome this deficiency. They must want to understand themselves, learn everything, think in advanced ways, and go as far as possible in school. Questions are never asked like: How are we as societies creating conditions in which children and even some adults feel unworthy, deficient, and not good enough?

Reason

The commitment to logic/reason that emerged from the Enlightenment is evident in our contemporary commitment to the scientific method, research as construct, and beliefs in concepts like cause and effect (however complex and indirect). Linear, scientific, gendered, and often dualistic logic has become so common that many in the Western world function as if there is only one really true, accurate way of approaching the world—and the West has found it.

As the preeminent scholar and individual whose work has been most often used to construct ideas about, and experiences with, children, Jean Piaget's theories of logical thought must be considered. Further, his work has been so far-reaching that even scholars who believe their work challenges his continue to reinforce much of what he assumed (Burman, 1994). Piaget's description of child illustrates well the Western commitment to reason, logical thought, and truth. Overall, his construction of child embodies the developing scientist. Specifically, the theory of equilibration is synonymous with the scientific method—beginning with a problem in understanding the world, various forms of hypothesis testing through exploration, and discovering how to understand and even solve the problem (Burman, 1994). Another example is the creation of the concrete versus abstract dichotomy that reinforces both dualistic thinking and the linear notion of reasoning from the simple to the more complex. Further, although Piagetian stages of development have been challenged by other developmentalists, the assumption of progress toward a qualitatively more advanced way of thinking has remained.

Directly attributable to Piagetian theories of logical-mathematical thought are the contemporary beliefs that learning is an individual activity that should focus on concepts and that cognition explains and should be privileged as knowledge more than the social or emotions (Silin, 1995). This focus has led to a distorted sense of reasoning for children. Studies of the way children approach and perhaps attempt to understand the world have been so dominated by logical mathematical knowledge that ideas like fantasy (Egan, 1988) and pleasure (Tobin, 1997) have been ignored, not to mention other possibilities. Powerful features of children's thinking, like romance, have been denied and even considered contaminants.

For Piaget, although he most likely did not recognize it, the generic developing child was male—a constructor, an explorer, an independent individual in control. "Even if he knocks the whole lot down ... It shows a baby he's in control and gives him his first feelings of independence" (Burman, 1994, p. 97, originally cited in *Practical Parenting*, September 1988). Reason and independent thought are emphasized throughout Piagetian theory, a perspective that places females in contradictory positions. While the ideal learner is described as using logic actively and functioning independently, females are often given contradictory messages. For females, social negotiation, compromise, and even passivity and dependence are encouraged by the outside world (Silin, 1995). Females may acquire this form of logical-mathematical reasoning but at the same time receive messages that girls and women are not best served by using this kind of thought (Walkerdine, 1988).

Closely tied to the larger Enlightenment/modernist agenda, Piaget constructed the concept of autonomy as the independent expression of logic and morality that considers others but is not controlled by them. The creation of such an individualistic construct as a major goal of development is imperialist because individualistic models of humanity are not valued by all cultures and societies. Further, by focusing on the individual, race, class, gender, and cultural inequities are easily denied (Buck-Morss, 1975; Sullivan, 1974).

In her extensive critique of the logic of Piagetian developmental perspectives, Walkerdine (1988) explains how his work reflects his belief in a rational, democratic society. Committed to the elimination of war, Piaget seems to have functioned with the belief that logical reasoning combined with moral autonomous behavior is the only way to attain and maintain peace. Walkerdine further proposes that Piaget most likely believed that he was contributing to understanding the free will and reasoning necessary for a rational, democratic society. However, his biases resulted in a theory that, like the construction of the orient to meet the needs and beliefs of the occident (Said, 1996; Viruru & Cannella, 2001b), created child to meet the egocentric, ethnocentric needs of the European male adult.

We must also admit that we understand why so many educators (especially early childhood educators) respond to the rationalist work of Piaget and developmental psychology. We have also supported (in the past) the ideas that developmental perspectives could save the world (especially the world of children). We know that many understand that the theories may not be complete, but believe that the use of them can improve circumstances for some children. After experiences from a wide range of cultural perspectives and circumstances, we now believe that, at best, the improvements attained from a developmental perspective may provide increased material resources and improved environmental conditions (e.g., materials for children to explore, increased range of opportunities, more adults available to the child). We also agree that improving material conditions is an accomplishment, but at what price—the denial (and perhaps even extinction) of diverse cultural knowledges, voices, and ways of being in the world? We believe that the imposition of any *one* form of interpreting the world on everyone (whether developmental or otherwise) is harmful to all of us ultimately. Diverse knowledges, different ways of thinking and being in the world, and multiple human voices and possibilities are ignored. We must also ask the question can we really improve material and environmental conditions for all human beings if we only focus on those conditions in the name of Western constructions of human change?

To further explain, Piaget took up the notion of child-centeredness that had been a key aspect of Rousseau's naturalism—including images of growth, freedom, interest, and activity. These perspectives are profoundly Western. Rousseau actually inscribed dualism by creating a counter-discourse to the interpretation of childhood as evil constructed by the Christian church; the dichotomous belief in evil versus good was still perpetuated (Cannella, 1997; Kessen, 1978; Weber, 1984). Piaget reinscribed this dualism by focusing on reason for the independent, self-regulating, acting child. Rousseau proposed that children needed freedom, yet his interpretation of freedom was the Western notion that would covertly construct a form of social regulation. "Let your pupil always believe that he is the master. . . . No other subjection is complete as that which keeps up the pretense of freedom; in such a way, one can even imprison the will" (quoting French version of Rousseau, 1933; in Singer, 1992, p. 130). Piaget's construct of child as individual, virtually ahistorical, and self-regulating (whether biological or otherwise) creates this same illusion of free thought. Yet this free thought is interpreted as following particular processes (at one's own rate, but processes that have been defined by Piaget) toward a particular rationalist way of interpreting the world. Critique of child-centeredness reveals a construct that is actually very authoritarian, perhaps even more than overt physical authority. Child-centeredness creates the illusion of freedom—the freedom to function and think in a theoretically predetermined direction and using Euro-American, male rationalism. For those of us who are not male, not White, not adult, not always labeled as rational must ask, how can this be freedom?

CHILD AS SCIENTIFIC OBJECT OF EMPIRE

The previous discussions have demonstrated the ways in which child as construct represents Western bias; these belief structures have also served to reinforce and privilege the ideas of scientific thought and universal, discoverable truths. The child, children, and childhood have embodied the acceptance of human truths, natural predetermined universals whose characteristics and very beings are believed to be revealed to those who are older with the right amount of well-conceptualized, objective science.

For many years, children were objects of Enlightenment theorizing and philosophizing (e.g., Rousseau). However, by the mid-1800s, child study placed them at the forefront of the belief in positivist science as well as creating them as the objects that would legitimate the emerging human sciences. Given credit for the first child study (although women had previously written their own sketches of infants), Charles Darwin tried to explain the difference in human children versus animals (Riley, 1983; Rose, 1985; Walkerdine & Lucey, 1989). Although Darwin did not use this work to directly foster hierarchy, the maintainance of the belief in racial superiority that justified imperialism (Burman, 1994) became a goal of the particular science (whether consciously or unconsciously). For example, in an 1881 article focusing on babies and science, Sully discussed how positivist science necessitated analysis of the simplist form of mind (quoted in Riley, 1983). These simple forms of mind existed in lower animals, savage natives, and infants.

The belief in childhood as truth and science's ability to reveal all aspects of that truth were accepted as givens. Science has been believed to reveal everything from the realities of physical changes in development— to constructions like bonding and attachment—to the appropriate roles of mothers and fathers in "raising" their children. For a complete discussion of the scientific child, see Burman (1994). Of special interest is the examination of the historical and political context of major scientific "advances" concerning child. These breakthroughs have often occurred at times in which one group of adults was attempting to control another and the belief in the scientific explanation of child facilitated the discourse of that control.

Women have most often been the object of control. For example, during World War II in the United States, women worked in all types of positions; they were even praised as completing work duties during a time of war. However, when the war was over and men wanted to return to work, social scientists began a public discourse filled with scientific claims that were used to control women as mothers. Constructs like "maternal deprivation" and "working mother damage to children" were widely used. The atmosphere created particular scientific beliefs that are even used against women today (Barber, 1943; Eyer, 1992).

Another more contemporary example is the discourse of child welfare in the United States that surrounded the 1996 reform efforts and the 2002 reauthorization. Data stating that children are better off with two parents have been used to push poor women toward marriage (Cannella, 2001). Unmarried women have been labeled incompetent, illegitimate, without morals, and responsible for all the problems in society (Cannella, Demas, & Rivas, 2002). They have been constructed as scientifically and, therefore morally, responsible for every aspect of the lives of their children.

Piaget believed in a scientific child who adapted and created concepts represented in science itself. Yet from within the same cultural context,

Freud created the scientific notion of child as created through sexual desire. Skinner created a scientific "baby in a box" (as cited in Kessen, 1979, p. 28). We would add that global, cross-cultural science has created all types of scientific children—those who are labeled as pathetic, who are not allowed childhoods, and even the disqualified, invisible offspring of "evil doers" (from the recent presidential discourse in the United States).

CONCLUSION

Psychology and science have created "children" as the perfect objects of Empire, those who would be defined, described, known, and controlled. We would suggest that Western, linear, deterministic power is both imposed (from the adult center) and exercised (as a network) on younger human beings. In the next chapter, we discuss ways in which a corporate institution for dealing with physical beings who are labeled child has been constructed using people like "experts" and constructs like "normality." This corporate institution that produces the methods for speaking about and seeing children is being disseminated over the entire globe.

5

CHILDHOOD AND CORPORATE STRUCTURES
OF CONTROL
Constituting Citizens of Empire

Childhood had become a primary locus of citizenship ... regimes for the reform of the dangerous child and rescue of the perishing child ... were imbued with an imperialism which envisioned as the highest aspiration of any child Anglo-Canadian citizenship in a Christian culture.

—McGillivray, 1997, p. 135

The testing of American minds has become big business, and is poised to become an even bigger business in coming years. . . . companies ... have set their sights on a potentially huge worldwide market.

—Sacks, 1999, p. 222

Just as Said (1996) has discussed regarding orientalism, a "corporate institution" has been constituted for dealing with those who are younger (p. 21). The corporate institution of child has inscribed ways of speaking about younger human beings, as well as cultivating ways of viewing, describing, teaching, representing, and ruling over them, ways of constituting ideal citizens for the Empire. Disregarding diverse ideas and voices, especially perspectives held by those labeled as children, corporate structures are now in place that maintain and even foster control. In this chapter, we explain these structures by examining: (1) the emergence of the human science disciplines that have created those who refer to themselves as expert researchers and practitioners regarding knowledge about human beings, (2) the inscription of particular predetermined characteristics on those who are younger as normal, rational, and developmental (e.g., needy, immature, innocent); (3) the overall legitimization of the rights of particular groups to observe, judge, and intervene into the lives of others; and (4) contemporary forms of representation that reinscribe colonialist power over the youngest of citizens.

CONSTRUCTING AND PRIVILEGING
EXPERT DISCIPLINARY KNOWLEDGE

As the emerging belief in science resulted in disciplines that were labeled hard sciences, fields with more social and people orientations also developed. These social sciences were proposed and constructed with the assumption that scientific truth about human beings could be revealed; further, the fields were legitimated using the same call for scientific "truth." For example, proponents and creators of the field positioned "psychological" knowledge, especially psychology of the individual, as revealing scientific truth about the nature of human beings. Psychology would be constructed, publicized, and practiced as the science of the mind, just as medicine proported to be the science of the body. An historical environment that assumed reason, dualism, and especially progress supported the beliefs that (1) the mind could be investigated, (2) those who were considered at lower levels (e.g., the young, the poor, populations identified as savage) exhibited behaviors and ways of being that had been overcome by the advanced, and (3) psychological (natural human) knowledge (truth) could be revealed through science. These Enlightenment beliefs were used to structure the questions for an individual psychology and established a context in which the individual mind would be both explained and held responsible and accountable for the conditions of life (Kessen, 1993).

Psychology, however, also arose at a time in which Europeans were greatly concerned about the "quality of the population," in particular, a time in which fear of "those sectors of society considered unstable and unruly" was growing (Burman, 1994, p. 13). Because the middle class believed that the poor were reproducing in larger numbers, the elimination of habits of poverty and the control of groups that were considered disorderly emerged as the discourse of the day. Although the nature/nurture binary had been invented by Francis Galton to describe the unchanging nature of human behavior, the notions were taken up and used to produce the field of psychology as science. The construction of psychological knowledge was embedded in the fear of contamination from particular social elements that would (according to the fear) permanently damage the dominant class.

Psychology, and to an even greater extent developmental psychology, emerged as a disciplinary field that was expected to explain nature and nurture, as well as individual and group actions from within an Enlightenment/modernist perspective. This scientific knowledge is grounded in the privileging of reason, dualistic thought, and placing human beings into patriarchal hierarchies. Those human beings who accept the knowledge and fit the mold are credited and rewarded, designated as normal and even as the expert. Those who do not believe that knowledge is truth—those who would suggest that psychology has emerged from a power-oriented belief in superiority and maintains imperialistic power over others—or who challenge experts in psychology—are discredited, blamed, and labeled as not scientific.

In many ways, although often well intended, the "expert" in psychological knowledge is the human embodiment of a controlling corporate structure. An authority for judging others, creating discourses about their lives, and intervening into the world of others has been generated. This corporate structure is found in the physical existence of many bodies—the psychologist, the child development expert, the educator. Even though these experts might disagree on specifics and even on the hierarchical position of their expertise, the superiority of the knowledge as scientific truth is assumed.

In discussing the notion of the "expert," particular understandings should first be acknowledged. In a dominant world (like the West) that has privileged the construction of knowledge (e.g., books, speech, technology), however socially constructed that knowledge may be, we must acknowledge that much information and many ideas have been generated. While we would challenge claims to truth and the authority created for particular groups over others in the use of those ideas, we would credit those who are actually informed experts as having worked to understand certain beliefs about the world. The knowledge should not, however, lead to power over others. We also understand that many who would consider themselves experts in psychology actually believe that they are standing for what is best for other human beings. However well intended or well informed regarding a particular socially constructed knowledge, continuous critique of underlying assumptions is necessary. The sharing of expert knowledge often places individuals and groups in positions in which they are labeled deficient and/or incompetent, resulting in feelings of abnormality and inferiority, silencing those who would attempt to share their understanding and generating public discourses and actions that have harmed large numbers of people (Bailey, 2002). By World War II, experts in psychology, psychiatry, and social work had created child as a univocal object controlled by those with appropriate expert knowledge (Jardine, 1988; Hawes, 1997).

To understand the notion of expert, simplistic interpretations—such as either crediting the expert with good intentions to assist others or critiquing the expert for creating power for a particular knowledge, group, or individual over others—must be challenged. The growth of the expert represents a form of complex control within the corporate state dominated by industrialization and corporate capitalism. The belief in knowledge as a source of power in the corporate state reinscribes that power to those who, through their economic position, determine what can be considered knowledge. As individuals become more dependent on the expert, antidemocratic tendencies result (Kincheloe, 1991). Personal authority is eroded by the creation of a pattern of dependence. Labeling the knowledge they have gained as rigorous and exacting, these experts are not often questioned. "Individuals depend on organizations, citizens depend on the state, workers depend on managers, and, of course, parents depend on the 'helping profession'" (p. 2).

A hierarchy of experts controls the industry of knowledge in the corporate state that surrounds child and family. As examples, parents, and even children themselves, have little voice in pronouncements about what is considered normal and adequate childrearing. The family, the child, or parents do not tend to be heard if their voices are not compatible with accepted expert knowledge. By the end of World War II, the cult of the expert in social science had been established. During the later half of the 20th century, a discourse in which child is understood as synonymous with development has dominated. Those who are part of the child development industry have attained the power (e.g., to judge others, to make money conducting trainings and/or selling materials, to obtain grants for studying children, to accredit).

Additionally, families have become the objects of those who consider themselves family values experts. This group of people uses the knowledge industry to create a desire in women for marriage, to foster the belief that children are virtually always better off in a particular type of family, and to narrow acceptance of diverse views of family.

The destruction of personal authority imposed by dependence on experts reflects the larger struggle in which "the modern industrialized, corporate state" has gained authority (Kincheloe, 1991, p. 2). Children and families are facing a form of colonialist objectification by the expert that repeatedly reinscribes scientific management of the knowledge industry over individuals, groups, and society at large. The experts themselves are even colonized in the process, resulting in the control of all involved.

PREDETERMINED NORMALITY

The belief that the contents of the mind can be revealed, especially for the minds of those who are younger, facilitates the expectation that there are mental and intellectual truths that are exhibited by a large number of people. These common ways of thinking have been labeled normal. Consistent with dualistic constructions of the world, when these mind truths have not been found, the results are labeled abnormal. This oppositional categorization of mind is similar to the classification practices of the British Raj in India. Using surveys, censuses, and ethnographies, the categories "British" and "Indian" were created and used to define the expected behavior of each (Cohn & Dirks, 1988). Even the defining of caste in India and tribe in Africa emerged as colonial constructs that maintained power for the colonizers. When people are constructed as static, as predetermined within particular groups (even if those people are younger human beings), social and political relations are confused and control is legitimated (Stoler & Cooper, 1997). The creation of the normal child (or a normal childhood) is another example of such a colonialist construct. Childhood is labeled normal or abnormal, as if there is a particular way of passing through the early years of life. Judgment and control over those who are younger is legitimated in the name of "normality." Both the normal and the abnormal are believed to be understood (even before they are born) and are thus controlled and limited.

Further, 19th and 20th-century western Europe was preoccupied (even fearful of) with what was considered the abnormal mental abilities of particular populations. The elitist's need to improve the quality of these abnormal groups lead to policy recommendations for testing children to determine and ultimately educate for and manage normality. Mental testing actually produced and reproduced the concepts of normal and abnormal, whether applied to children, people of color, women, or (and especially) those who had been conquered and labeled savage.

The normal/abnormal dualism depends on various discourses and institutions that facilitate its acceptance. Otherwise, conflicts with democratic ideologies would be obvious, rather than hidden. Testing, for example, is used to legitimate the dualism by invoking so-called scientific truth to prescribe and manage; because science is believed to at least represent progress toward truth, antidemocratic tendencies are ignored. Other examples include discourses of child guidance, particular education programs, and fields like child development and special education. Example institutions include mental hospitals, prisons, and some education settings. Notions of normality and abnormality are generated and perpetuated through these various sites of social administration and regulation (Burman, 1994).

Those who are categorized as children have been victims of this normal/abnormal structure of control in a variety of additional ways. First, they have been labeled as needy, innocent, and even savage. These labels, especially the concept of the needy child, have been taken up as the normal existence for those who are younger—as intrinsic to childhood. Regarding the construction of the normal child as needy, Woodhead (1990) explains the questionable positivist science (embedded in Western religion, thought, and male reason) that has created power for adults and objectifies those who are younger as without agency and living within a universal truth that is childhood. For example, research on childcare has assumed that children "need" one caregiver and has denied cultures in which children flourish with a large number of caregivers (Smith, 1980). Well-meaning child advocates have also constructed children as universally needing protection, a production of the norm that has been both beneficial and harmful. Protecting children from labor has kept them from unhealthy and unsafe working conditions, a goal that some of us might have for all working human beings around the world. However, we now understand that child labor laws and marketing restrictions have in some cases thrust families and entire villages into poverty as well as denied the significant social contributions that can be made by children. The discourse of need constructs children as passive and helpless, whether proposed as natural (needing love, security, experience) or psychologized science (needing social, emotional, cognitive support).

Often imposed on people of color, on citizens of countries labeled as "developing," and on women, discourses of normality oversimplify the functioning and life experiences of those who are normalized. Human diversity and uncertainty are concealed within the discourse. Universalist views of particular groups of people as ahistorical, apolitical, and acontextual are created. Further, focusing on normality such as normal child needs can actually privilege particular knowledges and skills while disqualifying others. The "social sciences" such as psychology assume that the truths that have been "uncovered" through Western perspectives fit everyone around the world. The recent international discourse proposing that all children need/deserve a normal childhood is an excellent example. The discourse uses an acontextual denial of circumstantial and cultural difference to mask the imperialism that has placed both younger and older human beings in poverty and limited life choices for everyone. The discourse even represents the so-called first world as the benevolent savior of younger human beings whose "savage" parents, communities, and "corrupt" countries have failed to provide the universal normal childhood (Burman, 1994; Nsamenang, 1992). Further, structures of corporate control are generated as interconnected and multiple with the inscription of normality/abnormality, which denies child/family/community knowledge and accepts the language and knowledges of experts (Silin, 1995).

A discussion of predetermined childhood normality cannot be complete without focusing on play, the construct that has been put forward as the child's work (as what is normal for childhood). This normalizing structure may be the most controversial. Well-meaning educators have accepted the psychological position that play is the normal behavior of childhood and that it represents the natural exploration, experimentation, and manipulation necessary for growth, development, and even health and happiness. Those educators and other psychologists and child development specialists feel that they must continually educate parents and others about the power of play (Dorrell, 2002). Play has not, however, been fully accepted by the public in the United States or in other parts of the world. Parents and others ask "When does the education program begin?" or state "All they do is play" (p. 75). Additionally, since play-based experts believe that play is for all those who are younger, they are understandably concerned when their contemporaries also question the concept of play. However, postcolonial critique requires analysis of all constructs, even those that would appear to allow freedom. We want to address the notion that in a variety of circumstances, freedom may only be an illusion that actually results in covert and even more effective colonization.

Play as a psychological construct was first promoted as an outlet for healing the emotions (e.g., see the works of Axline, Freud, and Erikson). Consistent with notions of linearity and progress, a variety of play theories have been developed that propose stages for advanced functioning as children become more mature (e.g., see the works of Parten and Piaget). Although embedded within beliefs that play is the activity of the moment that is satisfying to the child in the present, play has been constructed as the normal and natural way that children progress toward adult being.

However, the history of playlike behaviors in Europe, as described by Aries (1962), reveals the ways that play involved people of all ages. The European toy originated for adult rituals and pleasure. Miniature replicas of the real world, like dolls, were used by everyone and often created for such practices as religious rituals and to be placed in tombs. Although toys have been created for children younger than 3 years old for hundreds of years, before the modernist period younger human beings tended to join older people in play activities. Even games like tennis and hockey were played by joining all ages. When groups were segregated for play, gender and socioeconomic level were more likely to be the characteristics used (Hoyles, 1979).

Examination of play activities from diverse cultural perspectives reveals the Euro-American, middle-class bias in the construct. As examples, Heath's (1983) ethnographic work in the rural Carolinas of the United States with African American and White working-class cultures contradicts Piaget's description of infant play as concrete exploration of objects and repeated actions. The notion of sensori-motor play does not seem to fit the continued holding and cuddling by other human beings experienced by infants in the African American community. Rather than object play, the experiences seem much more tied to continued social connection. Goodwin (1990) also reveals the ways some Black children engage in verbal exploration rather than object exploration. Accepted theories of play have not, however, tended to address verbalization because of the assumed (from within dominant theories) abstraction of language. The examination of dominant constructs associated with play reveals that it is a cultural construction, a monocultural corporate structure that conceptualizes one way of behaving and experiencing the world for those who are younger yet disqualifies differences or contradictions.

Psychology has also resulted in the construction of so-called scientific truths regarding higher levels of play activity. To illustrate, dominant theories have considered understanding games with rules to represent advanced forms of play. Yet studies in diverse cultural settings contradict the advanced construction of complex hierarchical play behaviors. Heider (1977) explains the reaction of the Grand Valley Dani in Indonesia to a game introduced by teachers to school children. The game is called "Flip the Stick" and requires that an individual player use a long stick to flip a short one as many times as possible before other players catch it. The player with the most points (gained by flips) in the end is the winner. The Dani, however, do not believe in competition that would lead to winners and losers. Years after the game was introduced, observers found that it had been changed to a version that did not involve competition, winners and losers, or even record keeping. Values that underlie Western constructions of play and that have been assumed to be truth have been directly challenged by other cultural groups.

Additionally, the play/work binary represents Western individualized views of the world. These perspectives tend to associate play with pleasure and self-control, while work is associated with difficulty and as under the control of others (King, 1992). The separation of public and private, stressed to support the emergence of individualization, is modeled in the binary. At the same time, activities associated with pleasure (however constituted) and particular kinds of work are denied. These contradictions are placed in the margins just as the activities of children and the poor have been disqualified as deficient, immature, incompetent, and uninformed (Hoyles, 1979).

Using Western corporate structures, Hunt and Frankenberg (1990) illustrate how Disney creates and perpetuates the binary illusion. At Disneyland and Disney World, the visual focus on fun, play, and excitement so dominates that the workers (spending 8–10 hours on their feet in the hot sun) are invisible. Further, the visual illusion of play as universal and even equitable is created within the context of a prohibitive entrance cost; only the middle and upper class can afford Disney play.

One might propose that the notion that "play is the young child's work" provides a challenge to the play/work dualism; however, the idea actually fosters the corporate dichotomy. Binary interpretations of the world are perpetuated in at least two ways: (1) The separation between the child and adult is widened because child is grounded in the discourse of play while adults must function in the world of work. (2) Younger human beings are again treated as ahistorical, universal objects who are ignorant and can be easily fooled (into thinking play is work or work is play). Therefore, control over them and the environments in which they function is legitimated. This ahistorical, object view is challenged by both children and parents, even in dominant Western, privileged locations, as well as in diverse cultural settings around the world. For example, although enjoying the activities, children in U.S. kindergartens tend to label activities like painting and listening to stories as work (King, 1987). Parents ask about academic work expectations because both parents and children are aware of local contextual and societal pressures.

As we look around the world, play and work are not always viewed as separate concepts. In some contexts, there would exist no language constructs that distinguish the two. Bloch and Adler (1994) demonstrate how the experiences of most African children reflect a mix of activities, for example, using a stick to practice herding. Children in a variety of settings learn skills like blacksmithing by observing as apprentices and then practicing by beating on rocks (Lancy, 1984). While psychological experts in the West would most likely label this practice as the play behavior that facilitates work (the young child's work), the construction of two distinct constructs represents Western ideology.

The idealized version of childhood that is represented through play as natural and normal perpetuates the Western dominant ideologies that are hoped to ultimately prepare children to be like the more "advanced" Western male adult (Bloch, 1986). Play represents the biases and values of Western societies that privilege exploration with objects and mono-cultural notions of progress. The acceptance of play as a universal construct applicable to all creates a corporate structure of normalization and, consequently, labels for those considered abnormal because they cannot or choose not to play.

The acceptance of particular knowledges are embodied in the expert, combined with the reinscription of the knowledges through normalizing corporate structures (e.g., predetermined needs, natural play), results in the legitimation of power for particular groups over others. Surveillance and judgment of children and other groups who do not fit the structure are authorized in order to determine needs and to assess normality, for judgment, intervention, and control.

LEGITIMIZING SURVEILLANCE AND INTERVENTION

Out of this same Enlightenment/modernist/colonialist context emerged a European imperialism that included beliefs in European superiority as well as geographical physical conquest. Psychology, accepted as inde-pendent of political biases or purposes, was committed to a rigor that would be created through objective observations and measurement, which would then lead to understanding human reality, the "truth" for human beings (Broughton, 1987). Because psychology was constructed as revealing natural scientific truths, a discourse and practice of obser-vation and intervention were legitimated in the name of those truths. Further, since those who were younger were smaller, less experienced, and, most important, less likely to possess power, they were labeled as savage and primitive in thought, similar to the conquered who need to be controlled. Child study through observation was popularized in con-cert with the study of so-called primitive groups as subjects in the search for the origins and explanations of knowledge.

As individuals and groups were increasingly observed and their actions recorded, dominant beliefs in racial and gender superiority were fostered and imperialist actions justified (Burman, 1994; Gould, 1981). Observation was used to ensure correct habits—to avoid criminality and poverty. Further, this new psychological science based on observation also supported the newly constructed notion of pathological behavior in adults (Foucault, 1965). Observation was not simply the seeing of another that happens when human beings are in the same physical pres-ence. Observation, which sounds apolitical and innocent, could more accurately be termed surveillance because it has become an unquestioned method of categorization, judgment, and control. As explained in Chapter 3, surveillance developed as a disciplinary technology.

Today, modernist science fully accepts the surveillance of children in hospitals, homes, schools, and many other settings. This continued belief in surveillance is based on the position of inferiority in which children have been placed, at the lowest level of the patriarchal hierarchy. In the name of protection, needs, and growing knowledge, they are given no privacy. Observation is believed to be necessary as adults are told to have no blind spots in child environments, to enforce the ultimate pinoptic gaze (Foucault, 1977). Thousands of books are written on how to observe, assess, and judge children. Web sites contain instructions for everything from observing a child's ability to regulating sensations, to social behaviors like turn-taking, and to observing how a child functions in religious services. As those who are older, *we* certainly know that we would not want to be observed and judged regarding such a range of human experiences (although, we must admit that Western society is becoming the surveillance society). Some even approach child observation as a spiritual discipline. As with colonized peoples all over the world, children have had no role in the creation of these surveillance hierarchies or in the judgment and intervention into their lives that results (with the exception of those who learn quickly to see with the masters' eyes).

The gaze has been accepted as appropriate for all childhood spaces as a physical structure of power to be used over all children from all cultures around the world. Even in an age in which discussions of children's rights abound, surveillance has not often been questioned (James, Jenks, & Prout, 1998).

COLONIALIST POWER AND THE REPRESENTATION OF FUTURE CITIZENS

Postcolonial perspectives result in an awareness of the oblique and indirect ways in which power is used to control and colonize groups of human beings, power that may be exhibited by physical, material practice, but also through discourse and representation. There are a variety of contemporary forms of representation that create individuals and bodies as instruments of colonization—bodies that are local and bodies that are distant and may be represented as global. We believe that these bodies definitely include all those who are younger, not simply children of minority, marginalized, and/or physically "taken over" peoples. We include the entire group that has been labeled "child, children, and those engaging in childhood." Historical, contemporary, and even counter representations create this group of people as those who would be controlled.

As we discuss elsewhere (Viruru & Cannella, 2001), the idea that we should consider the possibility that all children, because they have become objects of our "constructions of childhood," are colonized is not a popular notion, even among some scholars who challenge dominant knowledges and truths. Objections have included the view that because children grow to become adults, they essentially outgrow their colonization. Others have pointed out that this perspective actually demonstrates the ultimate goal of colonization, one in which the colonized desires to become like the colonizer. Previously (Viruru & Cannella, 2001) we have discussed the ways in which the scientific construction of the adult/child dichotomy has (1) legitimated the physical occupation of the territory of children's lives by those who are older; (2) institutionalized the condition of need, thus constructing the rights of one group to make decisions for another; (3) actually continued a form of direct physical colonization through attempts to discipline bodies; and (4) fostered enlightened "knowledge" that represents children as those who must be taught to know (Western, adult information and forms of thought), by the colonizer who would give "children" a voice. As demonstrated at the beginning of this chapter, the construction of child can be juxtaposed with Said's (1996) analysis of the discourse of orientalism. The orient was a European invention comprised of exotic beings and landscapes. Those who are younger have been constructed through a similar lens, labeled "exotic" in their innocence, weakness, immaturity, lack of responsibility, and cuteness.

This postcolonial examination of child and childhood provides a vantage point from which to consider the notion of child in both the past and the present. Further, in the contemporary postmodern condition (e.g., questioning truth; bringing diversity, complexity, and ambiguity to the forefront), although many would continue to label this condition in which we live as *modern* (linear, industrial, capitalist power, patriarchal forms of reason), and, perhaps because of the *fear* of the postmodern condition, forms of reconstituted representation have emerged that surround the child. We believe that these ways of identifying and presenting others create power not only over those who are younger, but also over all of us. For this reason, we insist on a postcolonial critique of even the forms of representation that are used by perspectives that are more closely tied to postmodernism, as well as those that are more traditionally tied to modernist Enlightenment.

Ivison, Patton, and Sanders (2000), writing about the construction of political theory, have outlined three ways in which it has dealt with indigenous rights claims or the claims of indigenous peoples for justice: (1) The first form of action has been to require no real changes within

Western systems themselves and for those systems to hold fast to individualism and to noninterventionist approaches while ensuring that those cherished rights be extended to other people. (2) The second response calls for some reshaping of liberal political thought, but only to the extent that it continues to subscribe to the fundamental principles of equality and autonomy. (3) The third response argues for a much more radical reconceptualization of liberal thought, in light of the recognition that even such concepts as equality and autonomy are culturally constructed and thus necessarily limit values that cannot lay claim to any kind of universality or completeness. Those values themselves, to represent the kinds of ideas to which they lay claim, must be open to critique, deconstruction, and reshaping. As Young (2001) illustrates, this final method is very close to the aim of the postcolonial project—to create politics that are always open to critique.

As discussed in Chapter 3, the collusion of power and representation is perhaps best known through the work of Foucault, though we also acknowledged that he is not the only one to draw attention to this relationship. Stoler and Cooper (1997) explain how representation in the form of categories has been used by elites in societies to create power for themselves. This notion of representation through categorization is useful when examining contemporary discourses of child and how children are represented as static and powerless, even in the postmodern condition.

We are aware that for many people, representation has been, to put it more colloquially, the least of their problems. As Young (2001) has detailed in his analysis of the term colony, it mattered very little in the daily lives of people that the British did not regard India as a colony until very late in their rule or that Ireland was never a colony but represented as part of the Empire. (Categorizations were not made until late in the Empire.) Issues of representation, especially as tied to language, had little to do with daily existences and struggles for survival. At the same time, we are aware that imperial power, whether exercised over nations or over children, is facilitated though the institutions, ideologies, and forms of representation that it (Empire) creates (Young, 2001).

We would propose that children have become the unquestioned objects of (1) those who fear loss of power and challenge the diversity, ambiguity, and uncertainty of the postmodern condition, and (2) even those who engage in social critique in the name of possibility, opportunity, justice, and freedom (and we would place ourselves in this group). By various groups of adults, children are represented as everything from powerless beings who must be protected from the cruel world (whether that world consists of abusive parents or competitive corporations) to technological geniuses who understand abstractions in ways that most of the adults around them could not comprehend. We would also add that we could discuss the child living in the postmodern condition as representing a free agent in her or his world, after all, in the movies those who are younger are increasingly represented as sometimes even more intelligent problem-solvers than the adults; children are making financial decisions daily and influencing the purchasing choices of their parents. We list further how children are taking on (at young ages) the roles of the adults around them, potentially very decolonialist actions. However, to analyze childhood representation and colonialist power, we believe that the dominant contemporary discourses that govern identities and limit possibilities require more critical examination. We, therefore, propose at least four forms of representation that are reconstituting the construction of child, forms of representation that are much stronger and much more common than individual agency, advanced intellect, or decolonial actions. In our postmodern (yet modernist) condition, children are represented as: (1) an overt, accepted political tool for whom others may speak; (2) objects of moral theorizing and salvation; (3) the universalized global identity; and (4) representatives of a new hypercapitalism. These forms of representation place children into their "appropriate" positions as "citizens of Empire."

Children as Overt Political Tools

The use of plural language is a mark of depersonalization used on those who are the objects of colonization (Memmi, 1967). Perhaps there are few examples that make that case more clearly than the terms "children" and "childhood." The use of these universal generalizing terms is rarely critiqued as denying individual existences and agency; rather the terms are accepted as modes of protection and the assurance of certain rights and privileges. Our argument is, however, that such usage denies more than it affirms and results in the ultimate, ideal political tool.

James, Jenks, and Prout (1998)(1998) have pointed out that children are denied political power because they are created as an almost invisible category, subsumed within adult life. The unquestioning acceptance of the universality of the childhood experience has made it difficult for those who engage in the study of childhood to answer simple demographic questions about children's lives. Many government reports and the statistics within them are curiously devoid of children. Information about children's lives has been pieced together from reports that include children only incidentally (Overtrup, 1997).

"Children were, in other words, split up into categories that were not really relevant for our understanding of their life conditions; they were actually described according to adult conditions" (p. 33). Hernandez (1993) has shown that when poverty rates for children are calculated in terms of the number of adult parents living in poverty, the number is about 18%, but when children themselves are actually surveyed, the number is about 27%. The refusal to use children as the unit of account in social research is a statement about their political position, despite the widespread justification of political policies, in the name of children (James et al., 1998).

Probably one of the best examples of children's lack of political power and the ways in which they are used as political tools is the well-known saga of Elián Gonzalez. The remarkable lack of focus on Elián as a person and the complete appropriation of his identity, by both sides in the struggle, as a tool to be manipulated for their own purposes has been well documented (at the time of writing, the house in which Elián lived in Miami was reported to have been turned into a museum). For example, *Time* magazine, ironically calling him one of the people who mattered in the year 2000, described him in the following way:

> He was El Niño Milagro, "the miracle child." He was plucked from the waters, like Moses from the bulrushes, by a fisherman. He became known to us by one name. To have any greater religious overtones, the tale would have to involve visits from the Virgin Mary—which some said it did. And the standoff over what to do with Elián (now 7) after the November 1999 Cuban-refugee-boat sinking that killed his mother, was as intractable as a religious schism. To his father Juan Miguel, in Cuba, the Miami relatives who took Elián in were kidnappers, buying the boy's love with chocolate milk and trips to Disney World. To the relatives and their vocal, anti-Castro, Cuban-American supporters, Juan Miguel was a dupe or worse who sought his son's return to hell. The father talked about strafing his adversaries with a rifle. The relatives dared the government to take Elián by force. Finally it came to that: a predawn raid that produced dueling images—a terrified Elián cornered in a closet, a happy boy with his father. It is tempting but inaccurate to say politics simply overrode love in this case. Elián, it was clear, didn't lack for people who loved him. And love makes us do stupid things. (Diaz, 2000)

As a description of a person who mattered, it is interesting that this piece tells us almost nothing about the person himself. Issues like religion, political tensions, parental rights, capitalism, and the government's right to use force were all used to describe this "person." Who else but a child would be described as a compilation of issues?

Children as Objects of Moral Theorizing/Salvation

The recent focus on morality from both the left and right in the United States represents children (and all of us) by theorizing them as simple, uninformed, and lacking moral power or judgment. This moral deficit is addressed through fundamentalist theories of morality that would basically save children (and the world) from whatever "evil" has overtaken them. These theories are of "protection from evil" against everything from drugs, to the Internet, to kidnappers, to large corporations. Obviously, the September 11, 2001, attacks on the World Trade Center and the Pentagon in the United States fueled this theory of moral protection, providing circumstances in which a language of evil-doers and unquestioned unity have emerged.

As postcolonial critique and colonized peoples themselves have proposed, theory (and in this case, moral theorizing) has much more often been used to construct and solidify power over other human beings than to protect them. Western thought has "often embodied a series of culturally specific assumptions and judgments about the relative worth of other cultures, ways of life, value systems" and thus, despite its supposedly egalitarian roots, has often ended up justifying some "explicitly inegalitarian institutions and practices" (Ivison et al., 2000, p. 2). Statements like Marlow's in *Heart of Darkness* illustrate:

> The conquest of the earth which mostly means the taking it away from those who have a different complexion, or slightly flatter noses than ourselves, is not a pretty thing when you look into it too much. What redeems it is the idea only. An idea at the back of it; not a sentimental pretense but an idea, and an unselfish belief in the idea—something you can set up and bow down before and offer a sacrifice to (quoted in Young 2001, p. 25)

Perhaps we cannot avoid moral theorizing in some form. However, we are reminded of the need to be wary of privileging the "ideas" we are trying to create and to be constantly aware of the assumptions that cause us to create those ideas.

Postcolonial critiques of the representation of child as one to be saved could not be complete without mention of the institutions that perpetuate the construct. Education, as "ideological state apparatus" (Loomba, 1998, p. 31), is one of the most obvious examples that is implicated in the construction and representation of "child." A postcolonial examination reveals the role of education as a colonialist project that would save individuals (toward a salvation for lifelong learning, self-actualization, and scientific intellectual advancement) through the use of books and other material learning possessions. The more obvious tie between education and colonization is the physical control of the bodies of those who are younger; the bodies of "childhood" are only permitted to engage in sanctioned forms of pleasure, while spaces, times, and distances around them are compartmentalized, centered, scheduled, and separated (Cannella & Viruru, 2002). As Field (1995) suggests, there are no laws that protect children from the endless labor of education or the view of "mind" that dominates that education.

Children as the Universalized Global Identity

Holloway and Valentine (2000) note that debates about identity and difference have been a dominant focus of social science during the past two decades. Especially in fields outside of psychology, essentialist assumptions about identity have been challenged as understandings have increasingly focused on fracture, shift, and multiplicity. However, children's identities have not necessarily been open to the critique or the acceptance of multiplicity. Childhood has continued to be constituted as a biologically defined category during which children are expected to learn to be fully human adult beings (for a more detailed explanation of this see Cannella, 1997). This perspective has at times even been exhibited by scholars who call themselves feminists, postmodernists, or poststructuralists in relation to so-called adult identities.

Jenks (1996) discusses two strands of thinking that have dominated constructions of childhood—Dionysian and Apollonian views. The Dionysian view of children is that they are "little devils ... inherently naughty, unruly, unsocialized beings" (Holloway & Valentine, 2000, p. 3). This idea and Christian doctrine were closely linked to one another and were reflected in attitudes toward child-rearing for centuries. The Apollonian view of childhood emerged later, in the mid-18th century, and was formalized through the work of Rousseau, who celebrated the natural talents and virtues of children and saw them as "little angels." (The fact that Rousseau sent all five of his children to foundling homes introduces a major contradiction to the notion that he either celebrated children or thought they were born good. See Kessen [1981] and Cannella [1997]. Whichever construction of childhood one examines or accepts, both reflect an essentialized construction of what it means to be a child, with little room for complexity and change. Jenks (1996) points out that neither one of these opposing constructions is unproblematic, and that in some ways, both views are now accepted as part of an assumed universal nature of children.

We believe that both of these perspectives, as well as contemporary representations of child, result in the construction of human beings who are universal because they are without identities (in a time in which everyone is so concerned about identity—whether unitary, multiple, fractured, or shifting). For example, scholars like Joe Tobin, Richard Johnson, Chelsea Bailey, and Gail Boldt have suggested that nowhere in the discourse about childhood is there any recognition (other than as a behavior that needed to be sternly repressed) of children as sexual beings. Children's sexuality rather became one of the "discursive sites where bourgeois culture defined and defended its interests" (Stoler, 1995, p. 137). Further, children's sexuality became one of the "four strategic unities" that emerge in the early 18th century, where the mechanisms of knowledge and power centered on sex. The discourse of children's sexuality was founded on the assumption that although children were prone to indulge in physical pleasures, this was not natural. Therefore, parents, families, educators, and eventually psychologists would have to take charge. Such a construction allowed for more intimate surveillance both of children and their families. Middle-class parents in particular were denounced as the true culprits, in cases where children exhibited physical pleasure; lack of surveillance and lack of interest in their children was to blame, as well as parental tendency to entrust their children to domestic servants (Stoler, 1995). Stoler has shown how much of the 18th-century discourse about child-rearing centered around the dangers represented by wet nurses and domestic servants, who were seen as somewhat similar in that they both supposedly lacked self-control, civility, and restraint and thus were likely to engage in sexual behavior, unless properly monitored. Thus, the discourse of children's sexuality as improper behavior spawned a whole technology of power used to control children, families, and workers and to create younger human beings as without identity.

Darby (1997) sees the construction of the "margin" (an identity position in which children are placed) as a method through which dominant discourses legitimate themselves because the margin continues to be within the body of the existing discourse (contemporarily meaning "children exists because adults have power," which becomes "how do adults help children? control them? plan their lives?" and so forth). The margin exists within the body of that which already dominates. The constitution of the margin as the place from which diverse identities may emerge, in itself, denies identity.

The uncomplicated, marginalized, and even nonexistent identity ascribed to children is not an innocent practice, but one that is deeply implicated in the creation of technologies of power that continue to colonize and subjugate both children and adults. To further explain an already discussed example, the universal child that is known through psychology (however developmental, individualistic, or unique) creates children as advanced or slow, adults who are knowledgeable or uninformed, entire peoples who are enlightened or backward, and so forth. Finally, when the child is accepted as a universal, the knowledges, skills, complexities, and life experiences of both individuals and entire peoples (young and old) all around the world are denied, ignored, and disqualified.

Children as Instruments of Hypercapitalism

Finally, although we would question perspectives that represent children (and all of us) as innocent and unwilling victims of corporate domination, we must consider the contemporary, and perhaps new and even postmodern, form of capitalist representation. This hypercapitalism is a worldview grounded in the belief that money, markets, and power are synonymous and form the foundation for human functioning. Although an oversimplification, we can to some extent consider Euro-American history and thought (which has dominated the world) as moving from religion, to science, and now to capital as the dominant form of interpretation, representation, and power. This hypercapitalism has been constituted and gained a hegemonic hold as the corporate role in contemporary democratic societies has been reconstituted. Examples of these capitalist reconstitutions include judicial decisions that have redefined corporate entities as human with human rights, creating a type of super and immortal person with rights (Chomsky, 1999; Horwitz, 1992), and the construction of conservative corporate foundations with long-term extensive agendas that would reinvent academia, media, legislation, and the judiciary (Cannella, 2001; Covington, 1998). This hypercapitalism can be characterized by (1) interpretations of the world that are entirely based on capital, resources, and markets, (2) a fear of loosing material commodities, and (3) a belief that capital (rather than Enlightenment/modernist science) in now the solution to human problems. This lens has been most evident in recent calls to support "America" by going shopping and spending money. (The word America is in quotes because we prefer saying the United States since America is actually two continents much large than the United States with the name imposed by colonizers.)

Children (and by implication all of us) have become the literal representatives of hypercapitalism as they have been reconstituted as political
tools, objects of moral theorizing, and the unified, universal, yet nonexistent, identity that is used to justify adult discourse and action. What
better representatives than those who are not even given a democratic
individual voice (in representative governments)? Our Enlightened,
modern, and even postmodern discourses have conspired to create a
group of the invisibly colonized—those who are so dominated that they
are disqualified (without adult awareness) as human beings, those that
embody the successful separation and joining of discourses and material
practices of colonization. While we would not hesitate to stress that children themselves do not necessarily accept or function within this
colonization, we would stress the ideas that within the adult mind and
constitution, the colonization of childhood is complete and without
question.

CAUTIONS AND POSSIBILITIES

Young (2001) quotes the work of Bernal (1987) who suggests that in one
way or another all Western knowledge is a form of colonial discourse—
whether past, present, modern, or postmodern. Creating citizens within
Western discourse(s) and knowledge(s) may well be "constituting citizens of Empire," from whatever position or location. We were further
reminded of this possibility in recent televised discussions for Independence Day in the United States as American historians talked about the
work of the "fore-fathers" (labeling that is also disturbing) as intellec-
tuals who understood how to construct and plan for Empire (as if this
were good). Thus, as we consider the field of knowledge that has been
constructed around and purports to represent the lives of young children, we find it necessary to pause and reexamine our own postcolonial
critique as well as the dominant knowledge. How does our critique colonize? How does our conceptualization of corporate structures and
representations that colonized those who are younger actually limit
them?

Additionally, Young (2001) explains that colonial discourse analysis is
not the only medium through which the mechanisms of colonialism can
be understood, but it does provide a common ground through which
many disciplines can work. However, there is also a common caution to
keep in mind, "that all perspectives on colonialism share and have to deal
with a common discursive medium: the language used to describe or
analyze colonialism, which is not transparent, innocent or merely instrumental" (p. 15). Thus, colonial discourse analysis can bring to the

forefront the argument that colonialism was not just an economic or military activity, or notions like intellectual colonization, but we must remember that our postcolonial discourse is itself potentially, and probably, colonialist.

Further, Bhabha (1994) has challenged Said's central argument that in the case of orientalism, discourse was power by demonstrating the complicatedness of the relationship. Colonial discourse, Bhabha states, is often decentered from positions of power and authority and takes on such dimensions as hybridity and contradictions to further itself. Perhaps the most basic "tension of Empire" lies in the awareness that the otherness of the "other" is neither fixed nor stable but requires constant maintenance and definition (Stoler & Cooper, 1997). We would contend that this tension applies to those who are constructed as children, leaving them with avenues of resistance and agency. Finally, we would remind those "older" minds (however modern or postmodern) that have and continue to construct child and children—as other, as citizen, as less than us—that we can strive to challenge colonization, to denormalize, decolonize, and counter representation. We can join with those who are younger in a refusal to construct others as separate, lower, or not equal to us.

Part III
Possibilities from the Margins

6

RECONCEPTUALIZING EDUCATION
AS DECOLONIALIST PRACTICE

> Nietzsche argued in effect that first we make up our claims to truth, then we forget that we made them up, then we forget that we forgot.... To be subjected to education has meant to become disciplined according to a regimen of remembering and forgetting....
>
> Certain discourses of postcoloniality, postmodernity, and feminism have issued challenges, uncertainties, and complexities into critical traditions in education, thereby recasting the theoretical debate, revitalizing the political engagement.
>
> —Fendler, 1998, p. 61

Perhaps many who read a book on postcolonialism, childhood, and education would expect to find hundreds of pages filled with teaching techniques and practices that would treat everyone equally and result in "social justice and freedom for all." As is obvious by now, we believe that challenging colonialism, oppression, marginalization, and exclusion are much more difficult. The process is and will continue to be a struggle; the will to, and exercise of, power that is harmful and oppressive has existed for centuries and shows no sign of yielding. This power is most likely physical and hierarchical, as well as infusive and weblike. Further, processes and methodologies of decolonialization do not take a linear, goal-oriented, rationalist form. Decolonial possibilities can offer knowledges from the margin, unthought-of perspectives/life experiences, hidden histories, and disqualified voices as positions from which to reconceptualize discourses, individual values, and actions. However, decolonialist practice no longer accepts dichotomous thinking or predetermined action strategies; theory and the real world as recognized opposites (or other opposites for that matter); or, interpretations of the world that cannot conceptualize the possibilities for diverse knowledges that are the lives of human beings. Decolonial practice must be emergent while at the same time planned, must be individual while at the same time community based, must recognize dominant discourses while at the same time turning them upside down. There can be no models for decolonial practice because these models would most likely colonize. Decolonialism requires recognition of colonialism while at the same time challenging the dualistic thinking created by constructions of colonizer and colonized. We cannot provide decolonial methods or models, as we would surely then create for ourselves positions as colonizers.

We believe that shared vantage points can be created that provide decolonial positions and possiblities for us at this point in time. For the reconceptualization of education, we choose two discourses—one that has remained in the margin and therefore provides unique possibilities for the rethinking of what is important for education, and the other that has come to dominate both society and lives in schools without the recognition of the source and will to power from which it emanates. The first vantage point is that created by the multiplicities of feminist perspectives; these views create possibilities for rethinking the purposes and practices of education. The second vantage point is a view that would reveal the hypercapitalist network of power (the economic colonialist power) that is implicated in contemporary discourses and practices of testing.

We regret choosing very Western discourses for the generation of decolonial possibilities for education. We know that non-Western knowledges and possibilities are limitless. We choose discourses from the West, however, specifically in hope that our use of these can demonstrate how even enlightened modernism can be turned upside down to create decolonial possibilities.

FEMINIST PERSPECTIVES IN THE CONSTRUCTION OF DECOLONIALIST EDUCATION

The incorporation of feminist perspectives (there are many and they are diverse) in education would necessitate the acceptance of ambiguity, hybridity, complexity, and contradiction As Tong (1989) has said, "what makes feminist thought so liberating, is its vitality, its refusal to stop changing, to stop growing" (p. 237). Another reason that we believe that a feminist perspective is important is the inherently gendered nature of the field of education. According to Marsh (2001) although out-of-home childcare has been available to young children since at least the 17th century, discourses of gender placed females at home, centered in domestic activities. Girls were rarely educated beyond the basics of reading and writing. In later centuries, the philosophers credited with revolutionizing and revamping the field were all male (example, Rousseau, Pestalozzi, Froebel, and later Piaget). As Luke (1996) puts it, "the author-authorities of theories of childhood, motherhood and femininity have been men" (p. 169). Male discourses of gender have also placed women in positions in which we are responsible for all aspects of the lives of those who are younger: middle-class mothers have and continue to be placed at home to care for their children, whereas single (and currently perhaps women with grown children) middle-class women are placed in the role of caring and nurturing teachers.

Challenging Gender and Sex Role Stereotyping

Rensenbrink (2001) has drawn parallels between larger societal patterns of inequity and the practices that are prevalent in classrooms. In the 1960s women in the West began to question the naturalness of the roles assigned to women, and to see those roles rather as the result of expectations tailored by politics and other agendas. Questions were raised about the different amounts of attention accorded in academics: girls were expected to do poorly in math and science, and this was acceptable; but great concerns were raised about boys not doing as well in reading and writing. Even in a university community such as ours, the Radhika Virura's 7-year-old daughter, at the time of writing, is attending a summer camp on invention and creativity where almost two thirds of the participants are boys. Lee (2002) found that teachers in Brisbane, Australia, nominated as many as five times more boys than girls for a mathematics and science enrichment program for gifted young children. Walkerdine's (2000) study also underlines the contradictory images that are inherent in the ways that gender roles are created in early childhood education. In her study she discusses the behavior of one child in particular that we consider particularly interesting:

> Janie is six. In the classroom she sits almost silently well-behaved, the epitome of the hard-working girl, so often scorned as uninteresting in the educational literature on girls' attainment. She says very little and appears to be constantly aware of being watched and herself watches the model that she presents to her teacher and class-

mates, as well as to myself, seated in a corner of the classroom, making an audio recording. She always presents immaculate work and is used to getting very high marks. She asks to go to the toilet and leaves the classroom. As she is wearing a radio microphone I hear her cross the hall in which a class is doing music and movement to a radio programme: the teacher tells them to pretend to be bunnies. She leaves the hall and enters the silence of the toilets and in there, alone she sings loudly to herself. I imagine her swaying in front of the mirror. The song that she sings is one on the lips of many of the girls at the time I was making the recordings: Toni Basil's "Oh Mickie." (Walkerdine, 2000, p. 12)

As Walkerdine points out, whereas in the sanitized space of the classroom, this child presents the perfect image of the good little girl, in her private space the song she sings conjure up highly erotic and sexual images. Walkerdine's contention is that even by the age of 6, this child is aware of the kind of femininity that it is acceptable to portray in the classroom.

Stereotypes about women continue to proliferate in the literature as well as the images prevalent in popular culture available for young children. Studies have shown that in both fiction and nonfiction texts used with children, boys and men are the dominant figures. Analyses of history texts too have shown that whereas economic, cultural, social, and religious histories (often called women's histories) are often neglected, military and political accounts dominate (Walkerdine, 2000). Looking at the media directed at young children, Walkerdine found in her study of young children's use of computer games that boys seemed to prefer the apparent realism of fighting games. Interestingly, both boys and girls in the study were aware of what the concept of addiction was, but defined it very differently, girls tended to define it as how much one played games, whereas the boys defined it as being interested in violence. Scholars such as Luke (1996) and Seiter (1991) have looked at the gendered discourses that underlie the way in which space is organized in public spaces for children. In the era of hyper-capitalism, where chains such as McDonald's and Toys R Us are made to appear identical no matter where their location, gendered discourses have been a factor in determining their universal identities. Seiter's analysis found that at Toys R Us, high-tech toys and action figures were placed near the entrance (which were marketed to boys and fathers). Boys toys occupied the next sections and the girls toys were found at the rear of the store. Most merchandise is also color-coded according to gender, with metallic and primary colors signifying boys merchandise and pinks and purples indicating girls items. Furthermore, the girls' toy sections are surrounded by preschool toys and things for babies, suggesting, according to Luke, "a natural connection between real baby bottles, infant gear, cribs, strollers, baby buggies and 'pretend play' baby toys" (p. 172). The boys' sections, in Seiter's study, were next to the sporting goods and computer sections. Also, the boys toys tended to be more expensive and need more space to operate than the girls (for example, radio-controlled cars compared to doll houses). Not only does knowing about such circumstances sensitize educators to the world around them, but the information also suggests ways in which to look at our own classrooms and spaces. For example, Coffey and Delamont (2000) have indicated that playgrounds are spaces where girls can experience sexual harassment, as boys tend to dominate playground space.

Challenging the image or vision of the good girl, good mother, good teacher, good woman is crucial for educators. Both of us are amused at how much of our behavior, even as college professors, is dictated by these images that we have acquired, even though we grew up on different continents and continually attempt to challenge them in our own lives. Questioning goodness is difficult, but the kind of goodness that is predicated upon sacrifice, denial, and conformity cannot really be good, but represents rather another truth that has been made into reality.

Focusing on Girls and Women in Education

Stereotypic male knowledges and ways of interpreting the world have dominated classrooms in the West and are now proliferated around the world. Martin (1992) proposes that schools be centered around the 3C's of care, concern, and connection, knowledges that has not commonly been part of the curriculum. In a similar vein, Nel Noddings (1992) has proposed that school curricula should include what she calls "centers of care." Porter (1996) has suggested that part of this ethic of caring is a closer look at the concept of friendship, as research has shown that not only do women have more friendships than men, but the qualities of those friendships can be quite different. Similarly Woollett and Phoenix (1996) have shown how discourses of child development have constructed mothers as major sources of influence upon their children but have not paid much attention to mothers as a source of knowledge.

In a similar vein, recognizing the importance of respecting people's knowledges, Brady (1994) has said that a feminist pedagogy of elementary education recognizes the importance of students experiences in the classroom. Curriculum in such a framework becomes more of an empowering space where relationships can be defined and explored. Feminist pedagogies, according to Brady, legitimate personal experiences as a part of the curriculum and "insist on a wedding of affect and intellect" (p. 87). Such a feminist pedagogy also allows students (and we would add teachers) to come to "voice." Brady details how a teacher had students discover the writing in their own neighborhoods. As her inner-city students, in grades 1 through 5, took pictures and wrote stories about their neighborhoods, students became angry about the conditions in which they lived and wanted to take action. This curriculum, that Brady calls "without borders," is the kind of feminist pedagogy that we see as resisting colonization. Coffey and Delamont (2000) also emphasize the importance of respecting what they call "nonacademic" knowledges in schools. Paechter (1998) has distinguished between what she calls dominant and marginal subjects in the curriculum. She points out that subjects like home economics and physical education are relegated to the margins of the curriculum. It is not a coincidence, according to Paechter, that these subjects have gendered and social class histories (learning to cook and other such domestic knowledges are considered the province of working-class girls and manual labor too has distinct class-based connotations). Working these knowledges into the mainstream would seem to be an important task for feminizing education. The works of such scholars as Miller (1992), Grumet (1988), and Lather (1984) look at how autobiographical methods can be used to help women include their own experiences and representations into the curriculum.

Coffey and Delamont (2000) consider it important to employ feminist pedagogies in teaching children. One of the examples they point to that is particularly important is the practice of reading the subtext and becoming a "resistant reader" (p. 38). This practice suggests that teachers should actively engage students in challenging myths about male dominance that are so prevalent in texts. For example, in Vivian Paley's book (1997) *The Girl With the Brown Crayon*, children who were engaged in an extensive study of Leo Lionni's books, discovered that there were very few female "heroines" in them (Paley, 1997).

Recognizing How Teacher Work Has Been Gendered

Coffey and Delamont (2000) offer an insightful analysis into what they call the everyday work of teachers and how it has been structured through gendered notions of work as well as how feminist pedagogies can offer a way to resist this stereotyping. They suggest that one of the major tensions that women teachers experience in their everyday work life is that between autonomy and control. Autonomy for teachers is ensured by the layout of schools (where individual classrooms are usually isolated from one another). On the other hand, adopting policies such as standardized testing and national curricula presents a direct challenge to the notion of teacher autonomy. Feminist perspectives, however, have recognized that this kind of dichotomy is an oversimplification and even an illusion. The isolation that has traditionally been characterized as representing autonomy also ensures the vulnerability of women teachers. We read this not only as physical vulnerability, which is of course a concern, but also vulnerability in terms of responsibility. By denying teacher access to networks and communities in terms of their everyday work, their vulnerability and susceptibility to pressures too are enhanced. Acker (1994) suggests that this kind of isolation has made it difficult for teachers to organize and sustain feminist initiatives. However, as Coffey and Delamont suggest, most classroom volunteers and other staff in schools are female, which may be a place where networks can begin. Part of the everyday work of teachers also involves communication. The classroom is a place where much talking goes on, and teachers have an important role to play in "feminizing" the language that is used. Research has long suggested that classroom teachers spend more time talking to and interacting with boys (French & French, 1993; Swann & Graddol, 1994).

Apart from making sure that one is aware of how attention is being given and that alternatives are available to obviously sexist and gendered language, male-defined models of language and talk need to be challenged in more direct ways. Anzaldua (1987) has said that language is male discourse. Our previous work (Viruru & Cannella, 2001) suggests that silence as a way of communication has been challenged by male-dominated patterns of discourse, partly it would seem as silence does not fit the needs of capitalism (How does one sell silence?). Brady (1994) states that a feminist pedagogy of educating young children needs a language of "critique and possibility" (p. 94). As Brady and others (McLaren & Giroux, 1997) caution, language does not simply reflect reality but creates it. Thus, focusing on language as a key element in the ways in which gender is constructed is an important task for teachers. Authors such as Russell (1985) argue for the inclusion of popular culture in the classroom, which includes many examples of languages of resistance (the blue music form for example).

Coffey and Delamont (2000) also look at issues of discipline and control and how those can be enriched by feminist perspectives. We find the place that discipline and control occupy in teacher education programs particularly interesting. For most of our undergraduate students this is one of, if not their major concern. Many teacher education programs include separate courses on classroom management. What we find intriguing is how management has been separated from all the other processes that take place in a classroom and stripped of any connotation that would suggest that interacting with children involves a relationship, not the imposition of a management system. Gregg (1995) has also pointed out that many teachers are judged by their peers on their ability to manage their classrooms, rather than by their teaching abilities. This perspective reflects a gendered notion of what a good classroom teacher is (Davis, 1992; Shakeshaft, 1989), encouraging what Cunnison (1989) calls a macho culture of discipline. Thus, the issue of discipline and control is not simply about how to maintain order over children so that the work of the classroom can be accomplished, but about gender, relationships, and power. Paechter's (1998) study of classrooms points out that teachers tend to focus on overt disruptions in their classrooms (which are more often initiated by boys) and in some ways tend to reward or at least condone boisterous and competitive behavior. Girls in contrast are both viewed and rewarded for being passive and submissive. As Paechter points out, gendered notions of what does and does not constitute good behavior have multiple implications:

1. How teachers view problem students differs. Comments about difficult behavior in boys tend to focus on their behavior and academic performance, whereas girls are viewed in terms of their appearance and, if older, in terms of their sexual moralities.
2. Boys are more likely to be referred to special education programs or even to be suspended or removed from school.
3. The disruptive behavior of boys is more likely to result in lessons being geared toward their interests.
4. By focusing on overtly disruptive behavior, many of the problems encountered by girls are often overlooked (such as name calling, verbal abuse, and sexual harassment).

Pagano (1990) and Miller (1992) have both argued that for women in teaching, the conflict is not between their roles as nurturers and their roles as authority figures but rather with the power of overwhelmingly masculinist discourses that have separated the two. As Miller states, "these lenses often condense multiple realities into one unitary vision, thus distorting or even eliminating the experiences and expressions of many who see and live in those worlds differently" (p. 107).

Feminist Challenges to Teacher Education

Teacher education, according to Britzmann (1991) has become one of the "great anxieties' of the 20th and 21st centuries, as it grapples with the circumstances of educating masses of diverse populations. According to McWilliam (1995) teacher education is also viewed by many as related to the state of the economy, as parallels are often drawn between economic declines and the quality of schools and teachers. Coupled with this is a belief that more government interventions in the processes of education are needed, "in the name of greater accountability for diminishing resources" (p. 8). Scholars like Liston and Zeichner (1987) found that just as teacher educators tried to incorporate themes like language, history, and culture into the curricula, others reacted and even attempted to backlash by defining the problem of teacher quality in narrower and narrower terms (e.g., vocationalism, differentiating schools). A feminist approach to these problems results, as might be imagined, in ideas about teacher education that are radically different.

One of the "basics" of teacher education in the United States are the dualistic beliefs that one is either a teacher or not—student teachers are emphatically not teachers—and the great belief in the power of practical experience, the dichotomous theoretical versus the practical. As has been explored in earlier sections of this book, postcolonial theory is particularly useful in examining the effect that binaries have on our ways of functioning, pointing out how this kind of either/or logic denies the multiple states that individuals can inhabit at any one time. It also encourages teachers to separate things into clear categories (you are either a visual or auditory learner) and can cause them to get frustrated with students who do not respond to this kind of categorization. Coffey and Delamont (2000) look at this issue from a feminist perspective by examining how feminist analyses of becoming a teacher contrasts with mainstream ideas. Traditional approaches to teacher education have described preservice and new teachers as progressing through developmental stages to various levels of expertise, while feminist approaches have described teachers as continually grappling with issues of certainty, experimentation, and stabilization (Huberman, with Grounauer, & Marti, 1993). Feminist approaches have also focused on an often-ignored part of the process, how becoming a teacher is both individual as well as collective (Hatch, 1999). Marsh (2001) suggests that when one looks at the process of becoming a teacher as a social rather than an individual journey, it changes the way in which one approaches teacher education.

Another staple of teacher education programs in the Western world, as Coffey and Delamont (2000) point out, is the focus on "child-centered" pedagogies and the individual differences between children. We have already addressed some of the problems inherent in such a view in earlier chapters. However, issues specific to teacher education programs arise when this becomes the primary focus of those programs. Most beginning teachers are encouraged to consider each child as an individual and to avoid stereotyping. However well intentioned this might be, such an agenda tends to subsume issues of gender and social justice. When one refuses to see gender or race, although gender and race are major factors in the constituting of the individual to be seen, then we are not really seeing at all, just creating a version of the person in front of us that fits our own construction of the world.

Coffey and Delamont (2000) also address the issue of neutrality; the preferred position for many teachers is to remain neutral about society and education itself. Although the act of teaching is actually a political act, the system reinforces the illusion that one can be apolitical. The claim of neutrality actually perpetuates the status quo, increasing the likelihood that stereotypes, injustices, and biases go unchallenged. Coffey and Delamont see this kind of neutrality as part of the larger discourse of professionalism in education. This discourse of professionalism is once again male dominated, as it emphasizes competence, conformity, linearity, and protection of occupational autonomy. We ask the related questions: What would a feminist discourse of professionalism include? How would professional educators who would challenge patriarchy construct classrooms, schooling, and educational practices?

THE IMPOSITION OF TESTING: HYPERCAPITALISM AND CORPORATE COLONIZATION OF PUBLIC SCHOOLS

In the phenomenon of standardized testing, one sees not only the emphasis on scientific thinking, which is implicated in the past and continuing colonization of the globe, but also such influences as corporate capitalism, efficiency oriented approaches, and one very narrow view of childhood. Thus, a true understanding of testing and how it colonizes schools is crucial to building a critical consciousness about education.

Standards (that would be measured using predetermined test measures) have taken over public education in the United States. According to Meier (2000), in 49 of the 50 states, tests are administered in schools; furthermore, the new No Child Left Behind Act of 2002, which mandates testing in every state, is a particularly helpful example of how testing is implicated in larger societal structures. The process is based on four basic mechanisms: (1) Official frameworks are designed that describe what children ought to know and what they need to learn at different grade levels. (2) Classroom curricula (including commercial textbooks and scripted programs from textbook companies) are selected that are assumed to present the agreed-upon frameworks. (3) Assessment tests are designed and developed to measure whether children have achieved those desired standards. (4) Rewards are inflicted upon those who succeed and penalties those who do not. Schools are increasingly becoming part of an enormous system, heavily dominated by corporate interests, that relies increasingly on the most narrow "scientific" methods of test and measurement and the capitalist bottom line.

Every day stories about the influences that testing has had on the lives of children seem to abound. One hears of schools that no longer have recess or snack time, of kindergarten teachers who no longer teach units as the content does not prepare the children for the benchmark tests, of first graders who cannot read but are encouraged to learn how to bubble in circles to prepare for tests that are at least a couple of years away, of school districts that align their kindergarten curriculum with the 8th-grade test (even though it is well known that by the time those kindergartners reach the 8th grade the test would have been replaced several times), of schools that will be reconstituted as they did not meet the standards 3 years in a row, and of teachers who help their students cheat to save their jobs. "Most Americans take standardized mental tests as a rite of passage from the day they enter kindergarten" (Sacks, 1999, p. 5). Furthermore, test content and results have become an accepted truth by policymakers across the board. Republicans cannot be distinguished from democrats where the issue of testing is concerned (Kohn, 1999). The demands of the marketplace are even used as forms of legitimation because schools must produce educated people, which can be determined through test scores (or so the story goes).

The scenario continues with additional players who have their own agendas. In Chicago, for example, the number of children expelled from both elementary and secondary schools has risen recently. The reason for the expulsions is supposedly higher standards. The expelled children are sent to specially designed businesses for schooling, thus making expulsions profitable (Meier, 2000). As a result, however, test scores rose over a 3-year period buy 3.4%. But, in Lynnfield, Massachusetts, a program that ensured that minority children attended schools in affluent mostly White communities was discontinued as it did not help the school "raise its standards" (p. 4). The discourse on testing diverts attention from how schools are failing poor children especially from minority populations, from the inequities in school environments, resources, and opportunities provided to poor children. The imposition of standards that would be measured through tests has actually become an avenue for the maintenance of inequity (Ayers, 2000).

What Standardized Tests Do Not Do

When one analyzes the research on standardized testing that is not conducted by the testing industry, the results demonstrate that tests: (1) do not really predict later academic success; (2) are better predictors of a child's economic status than of his or her abilities; and (3) do not encourage what many scholars of education would characterize as meaningful learning (Sacks, 1999). First, the Graduate Record Exam (GRE), used by most universities in the United States as part of graduate admission, is virtually not related to performance in graduate school. Similarly, only about 16% of the variation in actual freshmen grades can be explained on the basis of their SAT scores (and that explanation could be because of the similarity in testing situations in college classes, not on content or skills learned). Despite this evidence, both the GRE and the SAT exams are entrenched in the American university system. "Scientific evidence," even when it is not evidence at all, is hard to resist. Further, this greater reliance on test scores denies women's achievements entirely because females tend to have better grades but lower test scores than males. Second, test scores, although only doubtful predictors of academic achievement and abilities, are strongly correlated with parents income and educational levels. Data show that for every $10,000 increase in a family's income, a child's test scores go up by 30 points on the SAT. Finally, tests "reward passive, superficial learning, drive instruction in undesirable directions and thwart meaningful educational reform" (Sacks, 1999, p. 8).

Kornhaber and Orfield (2001) analysed what they call the assumptions that underlie high-stakes testing and how many of those assumptions are false. They detail three assumptions they see as being particularly influential in maintaining the high-profile role that testing plays in American education: testing(1) enhances economic productivity, (2) motivates students, and (3) improves teaching and learning.

Regarding the link between testing and economic productivity, as Kornhaber and Orfield (2001) observed, despite the dire predictions of the Nation at Risk report, the U.S. economy actually pulled out of the slump of the 1980s and performed better than Japan and Germany, despite the low test scores of its school students. Furthermore, even if one were to admit that inferential statistics are predictors of future behavior, that would not support the connection between cognitive skills and economic productivity (Levin, 2001). Interestingly, Kornhaber and Orfield did find some studies (Bishop & Mane, 2001) that found a correlation between higher test scores (particularly in math) and higher wages. In other studies they also found that there did appear did to be some correlation between income and higher test scores. However, in the case of the Bishop and Mane study, what was significant was that for the Black and Hispanic graduates, these effects were minimal. Furthermore, as Kornhaber and Orfield point out, test scores are not positively correlated with the qualities that are commonly considered essential to job success (initiative, creativity, and reliability to name a few).

We find it particularly interesting that despite the evidence that test scores are not good predictors of academic success or job performance, the fact remains that students who do achieve higher test scores are rewarded in concrete ways (with college admissions and higher incomes). As we have pointed out earlier, constructions or views of the world become truths not because they are so, but because people choose to make them into truths. The question of why these correlations are made is something we will explore in later sections of this chapter.

One of the other common assumptions behind testing is that it motivates students to do better. As Kornhaber and Orfield (2001) put it, "common wisdom, as well as behavioral psychology, holds that normal thinking beings strive to gain rewards and avoid painful consequences" (p. 7). We find this comment interesting as it shows how standardized testing as a construct is related to the ideas of the Enlightenment and to the rational thinking individual use when making informed choices. However, as these same scholars point out, this reasoning is not as clear-cut as many would wish. As Madaus and Clarke (2001) point out, motivation is not a simple construct that can so easily be generalized across human beings. Furthermore, scholars such as Fordham and Ogbu (1986) found that children from historically subjugated groups are motivated in what might be called quite contrary ways, as they tend to identify with ideas that oppose dominant perceptions of success and values.

Along the same lines as Sacks (1999), Kornhaber and Orfield (2001) also comment on the common belief that tests improve the kinds of learning (however narrowly that might be defined) in schools. As these authors indicate, this is a very rational line of thinking; however, neither teaching nor learning "play out only in this rational and constructive way" (p. 9). As Madaus and Clarke (2001) state, whether or not it leads to improvements in teaching and learning, it certainly leads to more control over these processes. These authors have derived some general principles to describe the effects of standardized tests on teaching and learning:

1. The more any quantitative social indicator is used for social decision making, the more likely it will be to distort and corrupt the social process it is intended to monitor.
2. One of the necessary conditions for measurement driven instruction to work is that valued rewards or serious sanctions are perceived to be triggered by test performance. If teachers perceive that important decisions are related to the test results, they will teach to the test.

3. When test stakes are high, past exams come to define the curriculum. Once a high stakes testing program has been in place for several years, teachers see the kind of intellectual activity required by the previous test questions and prepare students to meet these demands.
4. When teaching to the test, teachers pay attention to the form of the test as well as the content. When this occurs, the form of the questions can narrow the focus of instruction, study and learning to the detriment of other skills. (p. 94)

McNeil and Velenzuela's (2001) study of the impact of the Texas Assessment of Academic Skills (TAAS) standardized test in Texas demonstrated that especially for children who were poor and for minorities, the curriculum was much more limited. All teachers, regardless of their subject-matter expertise, had to drill these students on math, reading, and writing. Furthermore, they found that under the TAAS system, educational expenditures were greatly affected, as "scarce instructional dollars" were diverted from enhancing the curriculum to test preparation materials and other such test-related items.

Testing and Education Practice

Most people would agree that testing is not appropriate for the youngest of students. Young children's minds are not considered "standardized" enough to measure up to the rigor of the tests. Yet, there is no denying that tests have had more impact on young children and their education than many would care to admit. In July 2003, President George W. Bush announced that he was trying to redefine Head Start in the United States so that its programs emphasized the basics of reading and math, and he held centers accountable for how much children learned. According to the *Washington Post*, this proposal could mean that children in these centers could be made to take standardized tests (Bryan College Station *Eagle*, July 8, 2003). On a limited scale, as Sacks (1999) has shown, children seeking admission to exclusive private schools in Manhattan are routinely subjected to tests such as the Weschler Preschool and Primary Scale of Intelligence—Revised (WIPPSIE-R) and Stanford-Binet Intelligence test. However in some states like Arizona, children are being asked to take standardized tests as early as the first grade (Ohanian, 2002).

On a more comprehensive level, Sacks has summarized the results of two long-term studies that look at the influence of a child's family background on standardized IQ test scores (the Children of the National

Longitudinal Study of Youth, sponsored by the U.S. Bureau of Labor Statistics and the Infant Health Development Project). Both these studies were started in the mid-1980s and gathered data over several years on thousands of children to examine the effects of poverty, family income, neighborhood, and ethnicity on cognitive development, which was measured by such devices as the WIPPSI-R and the Stanford-Binet scale for 3- and 4-year-olds. The results show quite strongly that "when it comes to scores on early IQ and achievement tests, *money matters*"(Sacks, 1999, p. 54). Long periods of poverty had a consistent effect on children's IQ scores and were stronger than any of the other factors being studied. Regarding race, the studies found that although there was a considerable difference in the IQ scores for Black and White children, these differences were virtually "eliminated by adjusting for differences in economic conditions and types of learning experiences" (Brooks-Gunn, Kebanov, & Duncan, 1996).

Ohanian (2002), in her book *What Happened to Recess and Why Are Our Children Struggling in Kindergarten?* provides an insightful analysis into many of the changes taking place in early childhood education classrooms across the country, as they labor under the shadow of the tests. One of the more compelling examples is the story of an elementary school that was built in Atlanta with no playground. The rationale given for this, to quote the then superintendent of schools in Atlanta, was "We are intent on improving academic performance. You don't do that by having kids hanging on monkey bars" (p. 2). As Ohanian points out, even the maggots that appear in Hollywood films are guaranteed a break from work, but children in American schools are increasingly being denied that right.

Ohanian (2002) also suggests that one of the reasons children in early elementary classrooms are getting more homework is because of the pressures put on teachers to raise test scores. Furthemore, as Ohanian stresses, the kind of skills that are being taught to children are cause for concern. She gives the example of a kindergarten benchmark from an elementary school in Honolulu; children should be able to identify the parts of a book (front and back cover, spine, title, and author). Other benchmarks include the need to access information efficiently and creatively and to use information accurately and creatively. This kind of language, as Ohanian points out, not only seems inappropriate to describe the work of children, but clearly reflects the business backgrounds that created it. In Texas, for example, although kindergartners are not given standardized tests, they are expected to meet specified benchmarks, and their progress is measured at several points during the year. The term benchmark was originally used by surveyors as something that was pressed into something like a rock or a wall to indicate elevation. However, this term is now used to measure educational excellence, especially in states that have heavily invested in testing, like "in the miracle state of Texas where every child soon will be above average in everything but housing, health care and books per capita" (Ohanian, 2002, p. 138). Later, benchmark became a term used by the software industry to measure the performance of a computer system. As Ohanian points out, after a 1996 Education Summit of governors, a nonprofit group called Achieve was created to help schools with their "curriculum requirements." Achieve's services are quite expensive, but the group does help schools find funding to pay their consultants (usually corporate funding). Achieve is cofounded by Louis V. Gerstner, formerly chair CEO of both RJR Nabisco and the IBM corporations. Achieve has defended the use of benchmarking to measure children's performance as an activity:

> That looks outward to find best practice and high performance and then measures actual business operations against those goals. Benchmarking in education follows the same principle. It is appropriate at a time when state education reforms are focused on raising student and school performance, as states want and need an external yardstick to gauge their efforts. (as cited in Ohanian, 2002, p. 140)

We believe that the benchmarking of children is an "enlightening" illustration of colonization.

Testing as Product of Corporate Hypercapitalism

Some would say that almost everyone in education dislikes testing; yet, the practice continues and is virtually becoming the purpose of education. Although this phenomenon is often seen as a mystery, further analysis reveals that at least one of the motives is profit. "Tests are enormously profitable for the corporations that prepare and grade them" (Kohn, 1999, p. 74). A range of companies not only market tests but also the materials that are designed to raise scores on them. We offer a brief look at the four major corporations that are involved in the business of testing. This analysis is provided on the PBS Web site at http://www.pbs.org/wgbh/pages/frontline/shows/schools/testing/companies.html.

> Harcourt Educational Measurement, whose signature test is the Stanford Achievement Test (SAT-9), currently attains 40 percent of the test-design market. Based in San Antonio, Texas, the company was

acquired by Reed Elsevier of London in 2001; Reed Elsevier sold Harcourt's higher education and business training to obtain antitrust clearance. Harcourt is involved with massive testing in Massachusetts (MCAS), Texas (TAAS), and Virginia (school certification).

CTB McGraw-Hill, whose signature test is the TerraNova (CTBS), currently attains just under 40 percent of the test-design market. Based in New York, McGraw-Hill also owns Standard & Poor's, *Business Week* magazine, and four TV stations. Nineteen states in the U.S. use CTB tests.

Riverside Publishing, whose signature test is the Iowa Test of Basic Skills (ITBS), was acquired by the French publishing and film company Vivendi Universal in 2001 when it purchased Houghton Mifflin, the parent company. Vivendi also owns Motown Records and Universal Pictures. Eight states in the U.S. use the test with over four million students involved.

NCS Pearson is the leading scorer of standardized tests. The London-based Pearson provides services to 15 states and scores tests for nearly 40 million students. In 2000, the company made $202.4 million on testing services.

As the testing company information shows, not only is there a great deal of money to be made from the implementation of standardized testing, but in all of these cases, testing is one corporate division of a larger conglomerate. Echoing many of the concerns that have been expressed earlier in this book, Giroux (2003) has traced the effects of the "narrow imperatives of consumption, privatization and the dynamics of the marketplace" on the sphere of education (p. 74). Public schools especially are attacked most vigorously, not only for their perceived failings (and their associations with women and children who overall are without financial resources), but simply because they are public and thus represent a huge contradiction to a world that is increasingly interpreted through a market lens. Schools themselves are being redefined by the logic of the global economy, becoming less and less concerned with teaching children and more and more preoccupied with the needs of "consumers." Within the past few years, business leaders and conservatives have managed to write the agenda, as schools have come to be viewed in terms of inputs and outputs, as being in the business of working with human capital, with teachers being the sellers of the product and the public school system being that ultimately deplorable entity—a monopoly (Metcalf, 2002), and a somewhat socialist monopoly at that. Concerns have even been raised as to whether the new sharpened focus on testing and accountability is part of a larger enterprise to do away with public schooling altogether (in Giroux, 2003).

McNeil (2000), in her book *Contradictions of Reform,* comments extensively on testing in the state of Texas and how testing is linked to corporate domination of education. According to McNeil, when the state decided to undertake a serious effort at school reform, it did not look to experts on education as to how to proceed, but rather brought in businessman Ross Perot to fix things. Perot's response was to "nuke" the system. According to McNeil, problems in schools were perceived as "management problems" awaiting the expert manager and as just one part of a larger bureaucracy. Thus, to fix the schools, one fixed problems in the bureaucracy, which was done by imposing strict management controls.

The impetus for testing seems to fit into a well-known corporate strategy; create a need and then try to fulfill it. As Kohn (1999) has shown, many recent reports on the state of American schooling have been authored by representatives of big business: for example, the Business Coalition for Education Reform, the Business Roundtable, the National Alliance of Business, and the Committee for Education Reform. According to Kohn, all of these reports use essentially the same terminology (overusing words such as tough, competitive, measurable, and accountability). Kohn underlines a point that is often forgotten in this analysis: businesses have very different goals from schools. They exist to provide financial returns to those who own them. Schools are not constituted for that purpose. Sacks estimates that children who entered schools in California in 1998 could expect to take at least ten achievement tests by the time they leave school. In Chicago, Sacks estimates, between the third and fourth grades, children might take almost two dozen tests. It is estimated that every year Americans take anywhere from 140–400 million standardized tests as part of their education and many more as part of business, industry, and governmental requirements (Sacks, 1999). Sacks estimates that by 1997, in the K–12 market alone, standardized achievement tests sales amounted to about $191 million. Executives at Houghton Mifflin have estimated that the worldwide market for preemployment tests is a $3 billion market, out of which 40% is in the United States.

Although creating and grading tests is a major part of the market, the testing industry has also spawned other branches. For example, according to Ohanian (2002), Kaplan Educational Centers (which is owned by the *Washington Post*) runs the Score! Learning Chain, charging $20 an hour for coaching, reinforcing, and customizing curriculum. According to Ohanian, this learning chain also hosts birthday parties where cake and ice cream are served after working on skills in targeted areas.

According to Sacks (1999) although it is well known that companies like Harcourt Brace own the Psychological Corporation (a testing firm founded in the 1920s by Edward Thorndike among others), which creates tests such as the Stanford Achievement Test and the Weschler Intelligence Tests, what is less publicized is how these companies use their entrenched status to their advantage. For example, when the state of California looked for a new test to adopt in its schools, it chose Harcourt Brace's Stanford Achievement Test. In 1998 alone, according to Sacks, this yielded $30 million in revenues to the company. Harcourt Brace is also expanding into the electronically deliverable employer test market. Although further details on how big businesses are profiting directly from testing are beyond the scope of this text, Sacks (1999) is a useful resource.

Ohanian has also shown how many corporations have expanded into the test preparation markets, even the ones who write the actual tests themselves (for example, McGraw-Hill sells test preparation skill booklets aimed at first graders). Others, such as William Bennett, the former U.S. Education Secretary, have announced the formation of online ventures that can grade practice standardized tests (for between $50 and a $100 per test) for parents who are concerned about test scores (Ohanian, 2002). Companies such as k12.com (which is owned by the Knowledge Learning Group, cofounded by the junk-bond king Michael Milken, and whose board members include Chester E. Finn and the media mogul Rupert Murdoch) also offer complete sequenced curricula that parents can buy for about $895 (Ohanian, 2002). Furthermore, in May 2001, McGraw Hill launched a teacher training program that is closely aligned with state standards and adopted textbooks (Ohanian, 2002). Ohanian also reports that Riverside Publishing (the company that writes the Iowa tests) aggressively markets its new assessment packages to public school principals, offering "deals" such as $31.56 to allow each third-grade student in a school to take the practice version of the test three times before he or she has to take the "real" thing.

Marshaling Resistance

Apple (2001) has said that "cultural struggles are not epiphenomenal. They *count*" (p. 195). As he elaborates, for groups that have power to retain it, large numbers of people have to believe that the version of reality they are being presented is superior to other ones. How they do this, according to Apple, is by "changing the very meaning of the key concepts and their accompanying structures of feeling that provide the centers of gravity for our hopes, fears and dreams about this society" (p. 195). In light of the above facts, we believe that to stand against testing and corporate control of public schooling is to resist colonization. We would like to present some examples of ways in which this is being done.

Actions for Classroom Teachers. A first step in resistance is to remind oneself that tests are not truths. Acceptance of this phenomenon is even more discouraging than viewpoints that defend them as legitimate measures of children's learning. Standardized tests, Kohn (2000) asserts, are not like the weather, something that people have no choice but to accept. "What we're facing is not a force of nature but a force of politics, and political decisions can be questioned, challenged and ultimately reversed" (p. 50).

Kohn has outlined what he calls both short-term and long-term ways in which tests can be resisted. For classroom teachers, he suggests that they do what is necessary to prepare children for the tests and then "get back to the real learning" (p. 51). He advocates sharing this policy with the family members of the children, explaining that the class needs to break away from its real purpose to focus on the tests for a while. This action is taken partly with the hope that parents will be moved to become advocates against testing as well. Kohn quotes studies (Daniel, 1993; Karnes, Shwedel, & Williams, 1983) that show that short intense periods of tutoring work just as well as long-term focus on the kinds of skills that tests measure. Kohn, however, does caution to make test preparation as creative as possible.

Since schooling is a political act and testing is complicated, choose an issue that might be open to debate and potential change. Such issues include whether tests should be the only means by which schools are evaluated; how often tests should be given; whether young children should be subjected to them; and whether they ought to be the kind of tests that compare children to one another (norm referenced tests) or those that compare performance to a predetermined standard (criterion referenced tests); and, whether children who are not native speakers of English should be given tests in English.

Long-term strategies include raising public awareness about testing, organizing letter-writing campaigns, organizing teach-ins on testing, creating bumper stickers against testing, and boycotting the tests. On a community level, Kohn (2000) suggests that each community survey its own schools and reflect on the impact of the testing. Guidelines for how this can be done are also given in his book. Kohn has multiple other suggestions for ways in which tests can be fought, some of which can also be found on his Web site (www.alfiekohn.org).

Apple (2001) also advocates for people with similar interests joining together. According to him, several groups, even though coming from very different backgrounds, have come together to fight the inclusion of Channel One in some schools (Channel One is a for-profit television network that now operates in thousands of schools across the country). Channel One gives schools free satellite dishes and VCRs and TV monitors in exchange for the right to a captive audience for a fixed amount of time each day. Their equipment is not only wired so that their's is the only channel that can be received, but commercials are a regular part of their broadcasts (Apple, 2001). Not only have groups such as Ralph Nader's "Commercial Alert" tried to combat Channel One, but the Southern Baptist Convention has passed a resolution condemning it as well as some conservative groups. These groups are also working together to oppose what Apple calls one of the "fastest-growing commercial technology initiatives in education": ZapMe! Corp., which provides free computers to schools in return for demographic data about students, which it uses to tailor advertising aimed specifically at those children. Apple considers the issue of testing one on which many groups can come together, despite their backgrounds, as the vision put forward by advocates of testing leaves so many people out.

Many efforts are already under way and some moderate successes have been gained. Parents and teachers have demonstrated in the streets in Colorado and Ohio, and lawsuits have been filed challenging the legality of the tests in Louisiana and Nevada (Kohn, 2000). Several individuals have taken strong positions against the way in which testing is being used. One of the most cited examples is that of George Schmidt, a Chicago public schoolteacher who published a part of the city's tests in a newspaper after the students had already taken them to raise public awareness about the issue (Kohn, 2000; Ohanian, 2001). He was fired from his job and also sued for over a million dollars

The Impact of Testing on Civil Rights. Huebert (2001) has looked at the issue of the appropriate standards in how tests are used and concludes that if these were enforced correctly, things would change dramatically. Drawing from various sources (especially the National Research Council study *High Stakes: Testing for Tracking, Promotion and Graduation,* the joint report *Standards and Educational Testing* report of the American Educational Research Association, the American Psychological Association and the National Council on Measurement in Education, also known as *Joint Standards*), Huebert defines three principal criteria for determining what constitutes appropriate use of testing: (1) measurement validity, whether or not the test is valid for the purpose it is being used for and whether it accurately measures the knowledge of the person taking the test; (2) attribution of cause, whether a student's performance on a test reflects knowledge and skill based on appropriate instruction or whether factors such as language barriers and disabilities have influenced the outcome of the test; and (3) the effectiveness of the treatment, whether decisions made on the basis of test scores are beneficial to the students.

As Huebert (2001) points out, if one looks at the issue of measurement validity, tests that are used to determine whether one graduates from school require "a close fit between what the test measures and what students have already been taught in the schools of the state or district that administers the test" (p. 183). However, such validity problems become a civil rights issue for many minority and English-language learners, who are disproportionately denied diplomas and placed in lower track classes on the basis of test scores. As Huebert and many others have pointed out, high standards cannot only be achieved by mandating tests; high standards require an equal if not greater investment in the quality of schooling and instruction (also called opportunity to learn standards). Regarding the attribution of cause criteria, Huebert explains that this is essentially a question of inferences and the interpretation placed on test scores. In many cases, the inferences are based on the assumption that the student has received proper instruction and that the test is an accurate measure of his or her knowledge, both of which assumptions, Huebert cautions, can be false. As the *Joint Standards* report cautions, "it is imperative to account for various plausible rival interpretations of low test performance such as anxiety, inattention, low motivation, fatigue, limited English proficiency" (as cited in Huebert, 2001, p. 186).

We note that testing as a construct can be critiqued from within modernism on the basis of validity, reliability, and so forth. However, further criticism is possible through postcolonial critique. First, testing assumes particular forms of knowledge and that the knowledges can be measured. Second, thinking (within such constructions) is certainly deterministic, assumes universals, and accepts labeling of the "other." Finally, testing has become an avenue for corporate capitalism, and colonialist control through market perspectives, domination, and material resources. Certainly, these notions represent the construction of Empire, and, hopefully, they are not the values that we want our children to gain through education.

7
CONSTRUCTING DECOLONIAL RESEARCH AGENDAS/METHODOLOGIES

"[R]esearch," is probably one of the dirtiest words in the indigenous world's vocabulary. Just knowing that someone measured our "faculties" by filling the skulls of our ancestors with millet seeds and compared the amount of millet seed to the capacity for mental thought offends our sense of who and what we are.

—Smith, 1999, p. 1

Viewed from a postcolonial perspective, research is not so simply, but complexly, another Euro-American, Enlightenment/modernist discursive practice that creates unequal power structures. Researchers attain power over the "subjects" of their inquiry. Construction of research that exists within the West reflects the modernist utopian beliefs that truth, reason, and science are paths to liberation, and that if we design our investigations appropriately and rigorously, we can truly "know" and understand (Cannella, 1997). We suspect that this liberation would be limited to the researcher and not the object/subjects of that research.

In response to such criticism, a range of researchers point to the existence of the constructivist/naturalistic/ehnographic paradigm, which is often interpreted as responding to concerns of liberation, voice, and representation. Originally conceptualized as the work of describing culture, ethnography is perhaps the most widely used form of research with people who have been historically subjugated and/or labeled savage, or the "wretched of the earth" (Fanon, 1963). The term ethnography is at times used to signify a form of social research that explores situations rather than testing hypotheses and interprets the meaning of human action. In contrast to more positivist or so-called scientific methods of research, ethnography has been adopted in a variety of fields concerned with the everyday lives and real world practices of human beings. Ethnography has expanded from its original base in anthropology to such fields as education. Currently, it has come to be accepted as a more human and responsive way to do research with children in diverse cultural settings.

Various scholars, especially feminists, critical theorists, and postmodernists, have, however, posited that although ethnographic research does not overtly belong to a deterministic framework, it continues to be hierarchical, undemocratic, and colonizing. The researcher maintains the power to decide whom and what to study and how to represent their voices. Ethnography has been critiqued as "fiction," a story that we constructed and that continues to be in the form of text and narratives, no matter who or what is being described. The people studied have rarely any voice in the shaping of how their stories are told. This issue is particularly relevant to people from diverse cultures, who if left on their own would very likely seek other ways in which to represent themselves. Ethnographic accounts of life in postcolonial countries or conditions (like African Americans in the United States) thus seem to unintentionally raise the question of whether research, as we presently conceptualize it, can ever go beyond colonizing people.

Other concerns about ethnographic research include its voyeuristic nature and the researchers "right" to conduct surveillance on other people (Walkerdine, 1997). Ethnography is part of a social science that attempts to get inside people's living spaces and "produce a truth about them," that gets a "voyeuristic thrill out of the 'oh, are they really like that' feeling" (p. 67). Reconceptualist educators have pointed to these colonialist problems in research with children by calling attention to participant observation as voyeuristic (Tobin & Davidson, 1990), the ethics of intervention during naturalistic inquiry (Hatch, 1995), and the determinism in conceptualizations of triangulation (Walderdine, 1997). Once again, the more powerful groups in society, armed with a seemingly infallible reason, have acquired the right to study and categorize "the other."

The issue of voice is often linked to the question of whose knowledge is seen as legitimate or valuable and informs dominant discourses. Colonizing discourses have created one group that is vocal (with voice) and the other that is silent. The silent group is defined in terms of what they lack; they are still somehow incomplete, and their deficiencies become the way to control them. When voice is "conferred" upon the "other," when "they are given voice," without recognizing or attempting to alter the inequities that created the original distinctions, the "giving of voice" or "listening to" just becomes another colonizing apparatus. As Mohanty (1991) explains, such constructions as voice also produce Western subjects as the only legitimate subjects of struggle, while those from the so-called third world are heard as "fragmented, inarticulate voices in (and from) the dark" (p. 42). Allowing different voices to be heard is not a solution, since it leads only to a unrealistic illusion of a harmonious pluralism. Such an approach continues to control people through modulating their voices and avoiding the conflict, struggle, and threat of disruption that postcolonial, critical dialogue could bring.

Finally, postcolonial critics point to the essential untranslatability of local discourses into imperialist language. As Spivak's (1988) classic essay suggests, speaking itself belongs to a tradition and history of domination. At best, postcolonial voices are translated versions of original thoughts. Gandhi's (1998) analysis of Seth's poem "Diwali" points out that for the poet, and for perhaps many others like him, an acquisition of the English language (or Western constructions of knowledge through research) is uneasily plagued by Macaulay's prophecy of "one taste / Of Western wisdom surpasses / All the books of the East" (Seth, 1981, p. 65). The final acquisition of such a voice, "to speak in the desired way," is to learn how to speak against oneself (Gandhi, 1998). As Seth concludes, one's "tongue is warped."

CAN THERE BE A DECOLONIALIST RESEARCH?

Based on the Enlightenment, universal, truth-oriented origins of research, one would feel compelled to believe there cannot be decolonialist research. Research, especially in the social sciences and medicine, embodies belief in truths, determinism, and legitimizing judgment of and speaking for others (whether the others are identified as backward and developing or as immature and growing). However, postcolonial critique (and we would add other forms of critical analysis) provides a perspective from which to turn research upside down, to reconceptualize, rethink, and generate a new understanding and practice of research that could join the decolonialist struggle. This conceptualization of research is not easily discussed and certainly does not fit with beliefs in models or preplanned controlled designs, because it involves suspending traditional understandings (to move outside of Western thought that has even created the boundaries that must be suspended) in order to consider possibilities. Because of this difficulty, we attempt here to describe a reconceptualization by using commonly understood categories for the discussion of dominant Western research. We know we are speaking with the master's voice (probably a voice that is also ours as educated, academic women living most of our lives in the United States), but we hope that the ideas discussed provide a challenge even to our use of the classifications.

Epistemological Goals of Research

As all of us are aware, the dominant Western goal of research is to reveal truths, or at least significant inferences, about reality (whether methods chosen are quantitative or qualitative); these truths are usually considered separate from the objective researcher. In recent years, epistemological perspectives that have challenged a will to truth have attempted to reveal constructions or interpretations rather than universal truths, therefore, denying a predetermined reality but invoking expectations for sophistication and trustworthiness. These more recent epistemological perspectives have opened doors to new and marginalized knowledges and ideas that were not being heard from the more positivist, linear, reasoned location; however, both sets of research ideologies accept the potential colonization of the research participants by the researcher (whether through categorization and labeling or through the power to interpret and, for both, place in print). Although most researchers recognize and claim that they want to improve society, this claim toward whatever form of utopia chosen by the researcher virtually always denies that research is a political, power-oriented act. (This is not a natural truth statement, but a remembering of the location from which the theory and practice of research originates.) Postcolonial critique (and various other critical perspectives) acknowledges the value structure that has been established by research (the forgotten biases of the Enlightenment and modernism) and does not deny its own biases. The purpose of postcolonial critique is social transformation for liberation and the continued remembering of the origins and politics of that purpose.

From our own readings of postcolonialism and postcolonial critique, we propose that research (especially for education and the social sciences) be reconceptualized with the following goals: (1) the pursuit (not as utopian truth, but as struggle for multiplicity) of social transformation for liberation, which includes contesting forms of domination, creating equal access, and generating political and cultural identities through collectivity, rather than coercion; (2) generating critical specific activism as collective transformational power (not as redemption or rescue for unfortunate or deficient individuals/groups); and (3) challenging the will to truth and power that legitimizes control for particular privileged people(s) and places "others" in the margins.

These goals require a critical disposition that continually challenges the will to truth and our acceptance of research methods without examining them for the tyrannies and oversimplifications of people that they create (e.g., measurement, ethnography, ethnology, surveillance labeled innocently as observation, classification). The goals are characterized by an appreciation for mutiplicity (of ways of being, histories, and methodologies), possibility (subjective generation of unthought-of ideas and revelation of hidden histories and power), and struggle (i.e., the recognition that liberation is complex, relative, and never fully attained). If research will be conducted, our memories must remain sharp, connecting the past and the present, or we will without realizing function from within the original values that generated the construct and practice of research.

The following questions can provide a critical disposition from which to function:

- Are we/how are we producing forms of exclusion through research activities?
- What is the position of privilege that is created by our unconscious ways of functioning that is/are Western and/or dominant (e.g., knowledge, theories, tools)?
- How do we pursue transformational liberatory research without imposing our (predetermined) notions of emancipation (i.e., our predetermined ideas of saving, as well as who needs saving, from what, and why)?
- How do we construct notions of research that do not imply inference? How can we question "knowing" itself as a purpose of research? Are there other questions we should be asking rather than "what do we know?"
- How do we critique our creation of research problems to insure that power is not generated for one group over another? (Demas, 2003, pp. 1–5)

Questions and Purposes that Drive Research

Obviously, when research is turned upside down and reconceptualized, the reasons and purposes for specific investigations would be changed. First, as one might guess, truth-oriented descriptions of how individuals/groups think, feel, and behave or experiments that would control and objectify would in most circumstances be totally rejected, accepted only as a challenge to previously imposed imperialist conditions. Liberatory social transformative goals require radically different purposes and questions. The following are examples of broad types of investigations that might be used to address a range of specific questions:

1. Investigations into how society produces forms of exclusion (for example, *Madness and Civilization* by Foucault [Foucault 1965] in which the societal construction of mental illness and resultant isolation is analyzed);
2. Studies that examine the reinscription of domination (for example, in examining a Hawaiian education program that uses Native Hawaiian elders as resources in teaching Hawaiian culture, Kaomea (2003) reveals how well intended, even progressive, programs can perpetuate hegemonic dynamics;
3. Research that reveals how the codes of imperialism are reinforced (for example, *Decolonizing Methodologies: Research and Indigenous Peoples* by Smith [1999] in which colonialist methods of research are directly examined—"feeding consumption, tuberculosis of the marketplace" [p. 102]); and
4. Indigenous (or marginalized) research agendas (for example, community action projects described by Smith [1999, pp. 123–141]).

Examples of further questions related to the areas above, but specifically tied to childhood and education are: "What are the ways in which early childhood curriculum reflects imperialist assumptions about and misrepresentations of historically colonized peoples?" "How do methods of screening, assessment, testing, and/or categorization of young children perpetuate the economic and social stratification of historically colonized peoples?" (Cannella & Bailey, 1999, p. 23). "How does one co-construct a new kind of research with children that reflects their perspectives?" (Viruru & Cannella, 2001b, p. 168).

Reconceptualizing Research Methods

Possibilities for research methods are broad and located across a variety of fields. First, postcolonial critique uses comprehensive analysis of the effects of colonization; the methods must be detailed and generate connections between the past and present. Second, a range of methodologies exists with the following being examples, while methods are also emergent and determined as the research progresses. Cultural studies, archaeological retrieval, and revaluation are methods that have been well used, with a range of examples available from a variety of fields (Young, 2001). Genealogical methods, used in a variety of ways by Foucault and postcolonial scholars, are widely available. Multiple forms of feminist critique are possible; for example, Angela Davis (in the foreword to Sandoval's (2000) book explains how U.S. third world feminism critiques the movement of power and constructs new vocabularies that decolonize the imagination. Defamiliarization is a method introduced by Shklovsky (1965 [1917]) that assists postcolonial scholars in "making the familiar strange" by revealing absences and erasures in teaching methods, curricula, and education programs (Kaomea, 2003). These methods are just a sampling of the possibilities.

Recognizing and Countering Attempts that Would Discredit

Just as Stoll attempted to discredit the work of Menchu (see Chapter 3), reconceptualized notions of research have already been, and will continue to be, categorized as not being research. Forgetting the truth that they have created, scholars from a range of fields invoke "objectivity, rigor, validity, standards, and generalizability" on forms of research they either do not understand or actually fear. Academic authority, the "struggle for interpretive power," and, of course, the rigidity with which a scholar educator approaches the meaning of his or her own work is at stake for some.

Those who would reconceptualize research must be prepared by creating networks of both scholar educators and community members, multiple forms of dissemination, and educational practices that support social transformation for liberation. New vocabularies, ways of imagining, and multiple methods for taking action must be generated.

CONSTRUCTING A POSTCOLONIAL RESEARCH ETHICS

We close this book, not with conclusions, but with a call for a postcolonial ethics regarding how we view those who are younger as well as each other, how we construct our educational practices, and how we conceptualize research. As teachers and researchers, we have functioned as if we were ethical because we "want what's best for children" or because we're "revealing silenced cultural voices." Yet, more often than not our beliefs and practices have been so familiar to us from within our Western, reasoned, privileged context that we have not been aware of their imperialist influence or the ways they perpetuate or create new forms of colonialist oppression. This should be our first concern, whether with research that involves public material or with research that directly involves interaction with other people. The ethical guide provided by the charter of the Indigenous Tribal Peoples of the Tropical Forests provides sound advice for the construction of research with those who are younger as well as those who have been considered colonized or oppressed. The guidelines include establishing research activities in which participants control their own unique knowledges, culture, and intellectual property, jointly control the research process itself, and are protected and have control regarding the dissemination of information (Smith, 1999). We would ask ourselves, how do we work with children and people who are not academically trained to ensure that any research we conduct on their behalf is in collaboration with them? If our goal is social transformation for liberation, a postcolonial research ethic, regarding what and who is studied and how, is absolutely necessary. Critiques of our own research before, during, and after the process should always ask: Does it lead to oppression or colonization? and Are we creating decolonialist possibilities?

AVOIDING CONCLUSIONS:
CONSTRUCTING DECOLONIAL POSSIBILITIES

We are steeped in our own forms of educated Western domination (whether as American or Indian), yet we believe that postcolonial critique offers possibilities for antioppressive understandings and decolonial actions that should be considered from positions all around the world. Our talk is embedded within the languages that are part of our personal, social, and professional lives. In some ways, this embeddedness limits the ways we can discuss and explain; further, it creates barriers (however individually) within which readers function. Again, however, just as postcolonial critique creates multiple sites from which we can view the lives of younger human beings (as well as ourselves), we feel that subaltern and other marginalized perspectives create unlimited possibilities for understandings and actions by all of us.

Additionally, we know that readers of this book may, even unconsciously, impose Western forms of dualistic reason on the content and ideas. People who are well intended in their philanthropic, pastoral, and intellectual attempts to "save the world" by making everyone like us will again say that our ideas are damaging to children. We are reminded of the colleague whose face turns red with anger whenever Gaile Cannella is mentioned because of past challenges to universalist child development. Others, who are perhaps less well intended regarding their own openness to the real impositions of power that have been experienced by those who are younger (as well as everyone else) will label our work as "not scientific" or "not intellectual" (therefore legitimating reasons for its immediate dismissal and disqualification). Classroom teachers, who are physically overloaded with intellectual, political, gendered, and market forms of imperialism that have been imposed on them and their students by textbook and testing companies, legislators, and accountability systems would most likely hope for direct actions that could change what is done in their classrooms, immediately, if not sooner. However, countering colonialist, imperialist actions is not easy or immediate; decolonialism requires recognition, disposition, actions, even temporary losses, and long-term struggle.

There are also people who may even understand exactly the complicatedness of postcolonial critique and simply believe that it is legitimate, or at least desirable, to have power over others. They may recognize that previously marginalized voices are now beginning to be heard, and actually fear those voices. Whether because of this understanding (and their fear of loss of power) or because of simplistic beliefs in superiority, these individuals and groups are the most disturbed by postcolonial critique. Some even take actions to create webs of power for themselves (as with the backlash against rights gained by women and people of color in the United States), and some move to create physical, social, and intellectual circumstances for the specific purpose of controlling and oppressing those whom they identify as the "other" (e.g., women and minorities who do not know "their place," children who through their very existence challenge the privileging of reason and linearity, anyone who would live life or create/interpret knowledge in ways that contradict universalist understandings of the world).

We hope that most readers of this book, however, are like us in that we do not want to claim to have right answers, correct knowledge, or accurate understandings. What we claim is that we are very concerned about the powers of oppression that have harmed and continue to damage and discredit human beings all over the world. We wrote this book because of that concern. We wanted to be humble and avoid being viewed as experts, while at the same time recognizing that the acts of writing and publication do not represent humility. We did not write this book because we believe that we can provide a postcolonial truth that will save the world (e.g., eliminate power over children, free the oppressed, or provide the truth regarding various other states that might be associated with the elimination of Empire). This book was written to share with you our own struggles as we learn and hear from the multiple diverse voices around the world; we have come to believe that postcolonial critique from multiple sites and related to multiple groups of people, knowledges, and ways of being in the world is absolutely necessary. For years, our personal and professional concerns have been for those who are younger, that concern is what actually created our need to conduct postcolonial critique regarding children and education.

We have throughout the book explained the basic concepts associated with postcolonial critique and how the constructions of both "child" and "education" are embedded within colonialist/imperialist practices, and would now suggest the following possibilities. First, the importance of *constructing a postcolonial disposition that embeds work with children* cannot be understated. This disposition would continually challenge the "will to power" that constructs younger human beings as the "other" and would not accept knowledges, theories, or actions in the name of "children" or anyone else that inhibits equal rights for everyone. This disposition would not accept sound bites, expert knowledge, or simplistic interpretations that oppress particular groups of people, placing them under the control of the more powerful. Narrow and stereotypical theories that label children (e.g., immature and requiring management), family (e.g., to be controlled by the patriarch), security (e.g., interpreted as power over others in the contemporary United States), our roles as human beings (e.g., women's dominant role as mothers), or any other control-oriented perspectives would be rejected. Second, *a major criteria for choosing knowledges/ practices as applicable to those who are younger would be an antioppressive, critical nature.* In educational settings, as well as other locations, knowledges that reveals histories and conditions that have and do create particular people as the "other" would be shared, studied, and understood. Further, liberatory knowledges that constructs possibilities for everyone, rather than creating narrowed languages and ways of thinking, would be privileged. Children would be encouraged to engage in continual critique of the situations in which we have placed them and others in contemporary societies; this critique would also involve local and global community actions determined by those who are younger in consultation with community members and cultural workers. Finally, *political, decolonialist actions would provide transformative revolutionary practice* in which bodies would refuse to be docile. Alliances would be formed that recognize the political nature of all human endeavor, whether as politics that maintains a colonialist status quo through inaction or as politics that learns about, reveals, and challenges webs of power that are designed to disqualify and marginalize particular human beings.

The actions that can be taken are only limited by the imaginations of people and the alliances that they are willing to form. We believe that it is long past the time to become revolutionary in our thoughts, languages, and actions—in the name of equity, equality, diversity, and the elimination of oppression tied to education, religion, economics structures, and other societal and even global institutions—yes, in the name of children and ourselves and because we want to eliminate elitist, imperialist oppression over anyone.

REFERENCES

Acker, S. (1994). *Gendered education: Sociological reflections on women, teaching and feminism.* Buckingham: Open University Press.

Alvarez, S. E., Dagnino, E., & Escobar, A. (Eds.). (1998). *Cultures of politics, politics of cultures: Re-visioning Latin American social movements.* Boulder, CO: Westview Press.

Amin, S. (1974). *Accumulation on a world scale: A critique of the theory of development.* New York: Monthly Review Press.

Amin, S. (1977). *Imperialism and unequal development.* Hassocks, UK: Harvester Press.

Amin, S. (1988). *Eurocentrism.* London: Zed Books.

Anderson, M. (1978). *The politcal economy of welfare reform in the United States.* Stanford University: Hoover Institution Press.

Anderson, P. (1976–77). The antinomies of Antonio Gransci. *New Left Review, 100,* 5–79.

Anzaldua, G. (1987). *Borderlands: La frontera.* San Francisco: Aunt Lute Books.

Appiah, K. (1992). *In my father's house: Africa in the philosophy of culture.* London: Methuen.

Apple, M. W. (2001). *Education the "right" way: Markets, standards, God and inequality.* New York: Routledge.

Aries, P. (1962). *Centuries of childhood—A social history of family life.* New York: Knopf.

Aristotle. (1941). Politica. In R. McKeon (Ed.), *The basic works of Aristotle.* New York: Random House.

Arndt, H. (1987). *Economic development: The history of an idea.* Chicago: University of Chicago Press.

Asad, T. (1991). From the history of colonial anthropology to the anthropology of western hegemony. In G. W. Stocking (Ed.), *Essays on the contextualization of ethnographic knowledge* (pp. 314–324). Madison: University of Wisconsin Press.

Ascher, M., & Ascher, R. (1997). Ethnomathematics. In A. B. Power & M. Frankenstein (Eds.), *Ethnomathematics: Challenging Eurocentrism in mathematics education* (pp. 25–50). Albany: State University of New York Press.

Ayers, W. (2000). The standards fraud. In J. Cohen & J. Rogers (Eds.), *Will standards save public education.* Boston: Beacon Press.

Bailey, C. (2002, April). *Bad moms in cyberspace: Performances of expertise in early childhood education.* Paper presented at the American Educational Research Association, New Orleans, LA.

Balch, S. H. (2001, August). *Rediscovering liberal education: A case for reform in America's universities.* The Insider, No. 286. Washington, DC: Heritage Foundation.

Barber, E. (1943). Marriage and the family after the war. *Annals of the American Academy of Political and Social Science, 229.*

Beauchamp, T., & Children, J. (1994). *Principles of biomedical ethics.* Oxford: Oxford University Press.

Bergum, V., & Bendfield, M. A. (2001). Shifts of attention: The experience of pregnancy in dualist and ondualist cultures. In R. Tong (Ed.), *Globalizing feminist bioethics: Cross cultural perspectives.* Boulder, CO: Westview Press.

Berry, J. (1997). *The interest group society.* New York: Longman.

Beverley, J. (2001). What happens when the subaltern speaks? In A. Arias (Ed.), *The Rigoberta Menchú controversy* (pp. 219–236). Minneapolis: University of Minnesota Press.

Bhabha, H. (1990). The other question: Difference, discrimination, and the discourse of colonialism. In R. Ferguson (Ed.), *Out there: Marginalization and contemporary cultures* (pp. 71–89). Cambridge, MA: MIT Press.

Bhabha, H. (1996). The other question. In P. Mongia (Ed.), *Contemporary postcolonial theory: A reader.* London, UK: Arnold.

Bhabha, H. K. (1994). *The location of culture.* London: Routledge.

Bishop, A. J. (1995). Western mathematics: The secret weapon of cultural imperialism. In B. Ashcroft, G. Griffiths, & H. Tiffin (Eds.), *The postcolonial studies reader* (pp. 71–77). New York: Routledge.

Bishop, J. H., & Mane, F. (2001). The impacts of minimum competency exam graduation requirements on college attendance and early labor market success of disadvantaged students. In G. Orfield & M. L. Kornhaber (Eds.), *Raising standards or raising barriers: Inequality and high states testing in public education* (pp. 51–84). New York: Century Foundation Press.

Bloch, E. (1986). *The principle of hope.* Oxford, UK: Basil Blackwell.

Bloch, M. N., & Adler, S. A. (1994). African children's play and the emergence of the sexual division of labor. In J. L. Roopnarine, J. E. Johnson, F. H. Hooper (Eds.), *Children's play in diverse cultures.* Albany: State University of New York Press.

Bloor, D. (1976). *Knowledge and social memory.* London: Routledge.

Brady, J. (1994). *Schooling young children: A feminist pedagogy for liberatory learning.* Albany: State University of New York Press.

Britton, C. (1999). *Edouard Glissand and postcolonial theory: Strategies of language and resistance.* Charlottesville: University Press of Virginia.

Britzman, D. P. (1991). *Practice Makes Practice: A critical study of learning to teach.* Albany: State University of New York Press.

Brooks, G. (1995). The hidden world of Islamic women. *Australian Magazine, 25–26,* 12–23.

Brooks-Gunn, J., Kebanov, P. K., & Duncan, G. J. (1996). Ethnic differences in children's intelligence scores: Role of economic deprivation, home environment and maternal characteristics. *Child Development, 67,* 397–408.

Broughton, J. M. (1987). An introduction to critical developmental psychology. In J. M. Broughton (Ed.), *Critical theories of psychological development* (pp. 1–30). New York: Plenum Press.

Buck-Morss, S. (1975). Socio-economic bias in Piaget's theory and its implications for cross-cultural studies. *Human Development, 18,* 34–45.

Bukharin, N. I. (1972). *Imperialism and world economy (1915).* London: Merlin Press.

Bulbeck, I. (1998). *Recorienting western feminisms: Women's diversity in a postcolonial world.* Cambridge: Cambridge University Press.

Burkholder, M. A., & Johnson, L. L. (1998). *Colonial Latin America* (3rd ed.). New York: Oxford University Press.

Burman, E. (1994). *Deconstructing developmental psychology.* New York: Routledge.

Burman, E. (1998). The pegagogics of post/modernity: The address to the child as political subject and object. In K. Lesnik-Oberstein (Ed.), *Children in culture: Approaches to childhood* (pp. 55–87). New York: Macmillan.

Bury, J. B. (1932). *The idea of progress: An inquiry into its origin and growth.* New York: Dover Publications.

Butterfield, L. H., Friedlaender, M., & Kline, M. J. (Eds.). (1975). *The book of Abigail and John: Selected letters of the Adams family.* Cambridge, MA: Harvard University Press.

Cabre, M. (2001). Toward a history of us all. In M. Mayberry, B. Subramaniam, & L. H. Weasel (Eds.), *Feminist science studies: A new generation* (pp. 120–124). New York: Routledge.

Cannella, G. S. (1997). *Deconstructing early childhood education: Social Justice and revolution.* New York: Peter Lang.

Cannella, G. S. (2001, May). *Child welfare in the United States: The construction of gendered, oppositional discourse(s).* Paper presented at the Restructuring the Governing Patterns of the Child, Education, and the Welfare State, Sweden.

Cannella, G. S., & Bailey, C. (1999). Postmodern research in early childhood education. In S. Reifel (Ed.), *Advances in early education and day care* (Vol. 10, pp. 3–39). Greenwich, CT: JAI Press.

Cannella, G. S., Demas, E., & Rivas, A. (2002, October). *Curriculum as public regulatory discourse: Using poor children to legislatively reinscribe heteronormativity and gender bias.* Paper presented at the Bergamo Conference on Curriculum Theorizing, Dayton, OH.

Cannella, G. S., & Viruru, R. (2002). (Euro-American constructions of) education of children (and adults) around the world: A postcolonial critique. In G. S. Cannella & J. Kincheloe (Eds.), *Kidworld: Childhood studies, global perspectives, and education* (pp. 197–213). New York: Peter Lang.

Cardoso, F., & Faletto, E. (1979). *Dependency and development in Latin America (1970).* Berkeley: University of California Press.

Carpenter, E. (1955). Eskimo space concepts. *Explorations, 5,* 131–145.

Castellano, M. B. (2000). Updating aboriginal traditions of knowledge. In G. J. S. Dei, B. L. Hall, & D. G. Rosenberg (Eds.), *Indigenous knowledge in global contexts: Multiple readings of our world* (pp. 21–36). Toronto: University of Toronto Press.

Cesaire, A. (1972). *Discourse on colonialism (1955).* (J. Pinkham, Trans.). New York: Monthly Review Press.

Chakrabarty, D. (2000). *Provincializing Europe: Postcolonial thought and historical difference.* Princeton, NJ: Princeton University Press.

Chaliand, G., & Rageau, J. P. (1995). *The penguin atlas of diasporas* (A. M. Barrett, Trans.). New York: Viking Penquin.

Chapkis, W. (1994). Skin deep. In A. M. Jagger (Ed.), *Living with contradictions: Controversies in feminist social ethics.* Boulder, CO: Westview Press.

Cheung, F. M. (1989). The women's centre: A community approach to feminism in Hong Kong. *American Journal of Community Psychology, 17*(1), 99–107.

Chomsky, N. (1999). *Profit over people: Neoliberalism and global order.* New York: Seven Stories Press.

Clarke, A., & Olesen, V. (1999). *Revisioning women, health and healing: Feminist, cultural and technoscience perspectives.* New York: Routledge.

Coffey, A., & Delamont, S. (2000). *Feminism and the classroom teacher: Research, praxis and pedagogy.* New York: Routledge Falmer.

Cohn, B. & Dirks, N. (1988). Beyond the fringe: The nation-state, colonialism and the technologies of power. *Journal of Historical Sociology*, (1), 224–229.

Coltrane, S. (1992). The micropolitics of gender in nonindustrial societies. *Gender and Society*, 6(1), 86–107.

Coontz, S. (1997). *The way we really are: Coming to terms with America's changing families*. New York: Basic Books.

Covington, S. (1998, Winter). How conservative philanthropies and think tanks transform U.S. policy. *Covert Action Quarterly*(63), 1–8 Retrieved January 24, 2001, from http://mediafilter.org/CAQ/caq63thinktank.html

Cunnison, S. (1989). Gender joking in the staff room. In S. Acker (Ed.), *Teachers, gender and careers*. London: Falmer.

Damon, W. (2000, June 19). Counterrevolution in the classroom. *Hoover Institution Weekly Essay*. Retrieved March 6, 2002 from http://www.hoover.stanford.edu/publicaffairs/we/current/damon_0600.html

Daniel, H. (1993, Winter). Whole language: What's the fuss. *Rethinking Schools*, 4–7.

Darby, P. Postcolonialism. In P. Darby (ed). *At the edge of international relations: Postcolonialism, gender and dependency* (pp. 12–32). London and New York: Pinter.

Darwin, C. (1859). *On the Origin of Species by means of natural selection*. London: John Murray.

Darwin, D. (1979). *The illustrated Origin of Species*. New York: Hill & Wang.

Davis, L. (1992). School power cultures under economic constraint. *Educational Review, 43*(2), 127–126.

Davis-Floyd, R. (1996). The technocratic body and the organic body: Hegemony and heresy in women's birth choices. In C. F. Sargent & C. B. Brettell (Eds.), *Gender and health: An international perspective* (pp. 123–135). NJ: Prentice-Hall.

De Alva, J. J. K. (1995). The postcolonization of (Latin) American experience: A reconsideration of "colonialism," "postcolonialism" and "mestizaje." In G. Prakash (Ed.), *After colonialism: Imperial histories and postcolonial displacements* (pp. 241–278). Princeton, NJ: Princeton University Press.

Demas, E. (2003). *Critical issues*.Unpublished manuscript, College Station, TX.

Demas, E., Cannella, G. S., & Rivas, A. (2003). Conservative foundations and the construction of public regulatory curriculum: Or methods that use poor children to legislatively reinscribe dominant power. *Journal of Curriculum Theorizing, 19*(3), 99–115.

Descola, P. (1996). Constructing natures: Symbolic ecology and social practice. In P. Descola & G. Palsson (Eds.), *Nature and society: Anthropological perspectives* (pp. 82–102). New York: Routledge.

Diaz, A. (2000). Elian Gonzalez. *Time Media Kit*. Retrieved July 12, 2003, from http://www.time.com/time/poy2000/pwm/elian.html.

Diniz, D., & Velez, A. C. G. (2001). Feminist bioethics: The emergence of the oppressed. In R. Tong (Ed.), *Globalizing feminist bioethics: Cross cultural perspectives* (pp. 62–73). Boulder, CO: Westview Press.

Dorrell, A. (2002). All they do is play? Play in preschool. In K. M. Paciorek & J. H. Munro (Eds.), *Early childhood education, 01/02* (pp. 75–77). Guilford, CT: McGraw-Hill.

D'Souza, D. (1991). *Illiberal eduction: The politics of race and sex on campus*. New York: Free Press.

Dunaway, W. A. (2002). Commodity chains and gendered exploitation: Rescuing women from the periphery of world-systems thought. In R. Grosfoguel & A. M. Cervantes-Rodriguez (Eds.), *The modern colonial/capitalist world system in the twentieth century: Global processes, antisystemic movements and the geopolitics of knowledge* (pp. 127–146). Westport, CT: Greenwood Press.

Egan, K. (1988). *Primary understanding: Education in early childhood*. New York: Routledge.

Escobar, A. (1995). *Encountering development: The making and unmaking of the third world.* Princeton, NJ: Princeton University Press.

Eyer, D. E. (1992). *Mother-infant bonding: A scientific fiction.* New Haven, CT: Yale University Press.

Faludi, S. (1991). *Backlash: The undeclared war against American women.* New York: Crown Publishers.

Fanon, F. (1963). *The wretched of the earth.* New York: Grove Press.

Fendler, L. (1998). What is it impossible to think? A genealogy of the educated subject. In T. Popkewitz & M. Brennan (Eds.), *Foucault's challenge: Discourse, knowledge, and power in education* (pp. 39–63). New York: Teachers College Press.

Ferro, M. (1997). *Colonization: A global history.* London: Routledge.

Field, N. (1995). The child as laborer and consumer: The disappearance of childhood in contemporary Japan. In S. Stephens (Ed.), *Children and the politics of culture* (pp. 51–78). Princeton, NJ: Princeton University Press.

Fordham, S., & Ogbu, J. U. (1986). Black students school success: Coping with the burden of "acting white." *Urban Review, 18*(3), 176–206.

Foucault, M. (1965). *Madness and civilization: A history of insanity in the age of reason.* New York: Pantheon.

Foucault, M. (1970). *The order of things: An archaeology of the human sciences.* New York: Vintage Books.

Foucault, M. (1972). *The archaeology of knowledge* (A. M. Sheridan Smith, Trans.). New York: Pantheon.

Foucault, M. (1977). *Discipline and punish: The birth of the prison.* New York: Pantheon.

Foucault, M. (1978). *The history of sexuality, Vol I.* New York: Pantheon.

Foucault, M. (1979). Governmentality. *Ideology and Consciousness, 6,* 5–21.

Foucault, M. (1980). *Power/knowledge: Selected interviews and other writings 1972–1977.* In C. Gordon & J. M. Marshall, K. (Eds.). Brighton, UK: Harvester.

Foucault, M. (1982). The subject and power. In H. L. Dreyfus & P. Rabinow (Eds.), *Michel Foucault: Beyond structuralism and hermeneutics.* Chicago: University of Chicago Press.

Frank, A. G. (1969). *Capitalism and underdevelopment in Latin America: Historical studies of Chile and Brazil (1967)* (rev.). New York: Monthly Review Press.

French, J., & French, P. (1993). Gender imbalances in the primary classroom. In P. Woods & M. Hammersley (Eds.), *Gender and ethnicity in schools.* London: Falmer Press.

French, V. (1991). Children in antiquity. In J. M. Hawes & N. R. Hiner (Eds.), *Children in historical and comparative perspective.* Westport, CT: Greenwood Press.

Frieire, P. (1973). *Education for critical consciousness.* New York: Seabury.

Furtado, C. (1964). *Development and underdevelopment* (R. W. d. Aguiar & E. C. Drysdale, Trans.). Berkeley: University of California Press.

Gandhi, L. (1998). *Postcolonial theory: A critical introduction.* New York: Columbia University Press.

Geertz, C. (1973). *The interpretation of cultures: Selected essays.* New York: Basic Books.

Ginsberg, E., & Lennox, S. (1996). Antifeminism in scholarship and publishing. In V. Clark, S. N. Garner, M. Higonnet, & K. Katrak (Eds.), *Anti-feminism in the academy* (VolS. 169–199). New York: Routledge.

Giroux, H. (2003). *The abandoned generation: Democracy beyond the culture of fear.* New York: Palgrave Macmillan.

Glider, G. (1981). *Wealth and poverty.* San Francisco: Institute for Contemporary Studies.

Goodwin, M. H. (1990). *He said/she said: Talk as social organization among black children.* Bloomington: Indiana University Press.

Gordon, C. (1991). Governmental rationality: An introduction. In G. Burchell, C. Gordon, &

P. Miller (Eds.), *The Foucault effect: Studies in governmentality* (pp. 1–52). Chicago: University of Chicago Press.

Gordon, L. (1990). *Woman's body, woman's right: Birth control in America.* New York: Pergamon Press.

Gould, S. J. (1981). *The mismeasure of man.* New York: W. W. Norton.

Graff, H. J. (2001). Literacy's myths and legacies: From lessons from the history of literacy to the question of critical literacy. In P. Freebody, S. Muspratt, B. Dwyer (Eds.), *Difference, silence and textual practive: Studies in critical literacy* (pp. 1–30). Creskill, NJ: Hampton Press.

Gramsci, A. (1971). *Selections from prison notebooks* (Q. Hoare & G. N. Smith, Trans.). London: Lawrence & Wishart.

Greer, G. (1984). *Sex and destiny: The politics of human fertility.* New York: Harper & Row.

Gregg, J. (1995). Discipline, control and the school tradition. *Teaching and Teacher Education, 11*(6), 579–594.

Grosfoguel, R., & Cervantes-Rodriguez, A. M. (2002). Introduction: Unthinking twentieth century Eurocentric mythologies: Universal knowledge, decolonization and developmentalism. In R. Grosfoguel & A. M. Cervantes-Rodriguez (Eds.), *The modern colonial/capitalist world system in the twentieth century: Global processes, antisystemic movements and the geopolitics of knowledge* (Vols. 11–30). Westport, CT: Greenwood Press.

Grossman, Z. (1994, March). Erecting the new wall: Geopolitics and the restructuring of Europe. *Z Magazine, March,* 39–45.

Grumet, M. R. (1988). *Bitter milk: Women and teaching.* Amherst, MA: University of Massachusetts Press.

Guha, R. (1988). The prose of counter-insurgency. In R. Guha & G. Spivak (Eds.), *Selected subaltern studies.* New York: Oxford University Press.

Hadjor, K. B. (1993). *The Penguin dictionary of third world terms.* London: Penguin.

Haraway, D. (1989). *Primate visions: Gender, race, and nature in the world of modern science.* London, UK: Verso.

Harding, S. (1998). *Is science multicultural: Postcolonialsums, feminisms and epistemologies.* Bloomington: Indiana University Press.

Haskins, R., Sawhill, I., & Weaver, K. (2001, January). Welfare reform reauthorization; An overview of problems and issues. *Brookings Institute.* Retrieved March 15, 2001 from http://www.brookings.edu.

Hatch, A. J. (1995). Ethical conflicts in classroom research: Examples from a study of peer stigmatization in kindergarten. In A. J. Hatch (Ed.), *Qualitative research in early childhood settings* (pp. 63–78). Westport, CT: Praeger.

Hatch, A. J. (1999). What preservice teachers can learn from studies of teachers' work. *Teaching and Teacher Education, 15*(3), 229–242.

Havinden, M., & Meredith, D. (1993). *Colonialism and development: Britain and its tropical colonies, 1850–1960.* London: Routledge.

Hawes, J. M. (1997). *Children between the wars: American childhood (1920–40).* New York: Twayne.

Heath, S. B. (1983). *Ways with words: Language, life, and work in communities and classrooms.* Cambridge, UK: Cambridge University Press.

Heider, K. G. (1977). From Javanese to Dani: The translation of a game. In P. Stevens (Ed.), *Studies in the anthropology of play.* West Point, NY: Leisure Press.

Henry, E. (2001). Towards a feeling for the organism. In M. Mayberry, B. Subramaniam, L. H. Weasel (Eds.), *Feminist science studies: A new generation* (pp. 87–92). New York: Routledge.

Hernandez, D. L. (1993). *America's children: Resources from family, government, and economy.* New York: Russell Sage Foundation.

Holloway, S., & Valentine, G. (2000). Corked hats and coronation street: British and New Zealand children's imaginative geographies of the Other. *Childhood: A Global Journal of Child Research, 7*(3), 335–357.

hooks, b. (1994). *Outlaw culture: Resisting representations.* New York: Routledge.

hooks, b. (2000). *Feminism is for everybody: Passionate politics.* Cambridge, MA: South End Press.

Horwitz, M. (1992). *The transformation of American law, 1870–1960.* Cambridge, MA: Harvard University Press.

Howell, S. (1996). Nature in culture or culture in nature? Chewong ideas of "humans" and other species. In P. Descola & G. Palsson (Eds.), *Nature and society: Anthropological perspectives* (pp. 127–144). New York: Routledge.

Hoyles, M. (1979). *Changing childhood.* London, UK: Writers and Readers Publishing Cooperative.

Huberman, M., with Grounauer, M., & Marti, J. (1993). *The lives of teachers.* New York: Teachers College Press.

Huebert, P. (2001). High stakes testing and civil rights: Standards of appropriate test use and a strategy for enforcing them. In G. Orfield & M. L. Kornhaber (Eds.), *Raising standards or raising barriers: Inequality and high stakes testing in public education* (pp. 179–194). New York: Century Foundation Press.

Hunt, P., & Frankenberg, R. (1990). It's a small world: Disneyland, the family and the multiple re-presentations of American child. In A. James & A. Prout (Eds.), *Constructing and reconstructing childhood.* London, UK: Falmer Press.

Ingold, T. (1996). *The forager and economic man.* In P. Descola & G. Palsson (Eds.), *Nature and society: Anthropological perspectives* (pp. 25–44). New York: Routledge.

Ivison, D., Patton, P., & Sanders, W. (2000). Introduction. In D. Ivison, P. Patton, W. Sanders (Eds.), *Political theory and the rights of indigenous peoples* (pp. 1–24). Cambridge: Cambridge University Press.

Jaimes, M. A., & Halsey, T. (1997). American Indian women: At the center of indigenous resistance in contemporary North America. In A. McClintock, A. Mufti, & E. Shohat (Eds.), *Dangerous liasons: Gender, nation and postcolonialperpsectives* (pp. 61–82). Minneapolis: University of Minnesota Press.

James, A., Jenks, C., & Prout, A. (1998). *Theorizing childhood.* New York: Teachers College Press.

JanMohamed, A. R. (1985). The economy of Manichean allegory: The function of racial difference in colonialist literature. *Critical Inquiry, 12,* 59–87.

Jardine, D. (1988). There are children all around us. *Journal of Educational Thought, 22,* 178–186.

Jenks, C. (1996). *Childhood.* London: Routledge.

Jones, S. (1993). Gender and rationality among Arab families in Lebanon. *Feminist Studies, 19*(3), 465–486.

Joseph, G. G. (1997). Foundations of eurocentrism in mathematics. In A. B. Power & M. Frankenstein (Eds.), *Ethnomathematics: Challenging Eurocentrism in mathematics education* (Vol. 61–82). Albany: State University of New York Press.

Jung, C. G., & Kerenyi, C. (1963). *Essays on a science of mythology: The myth of divine child and the mysteries of eleusis.* Princeton, NJ: Princeton University Press.

Kaomea, J. (2003). Reading erasures and making the familiar strange: Defamiliarizing methods for research in formerly colonized and historically oppressed communities. *Educational Researcher, 32*(2), 14–25.

Karnes, M. B., Shwedel, A. M., & Williams, M. B. (1983). A comparison of five approaches for educating children from low income homes. In C. f. L. Studies (Ed.), *As the twig is bent, lasting effects of preschool programs.* Hillsdale, NJ: L. Erlbaum Associates.

Kennedy, D. (1988). Images of the young child in hostory: Enlightenment and romance. *Early Childhood Researach Quarterly, 3,* 121–137.

Kessen, W. (1978). Rousseau's children. *Daedalus, 107*(3), 155–165.

Kessen, W. (1979). The American child and other cultural inventions. *American Psychologist, 34,* 815–820.

Kessen, W. (1981). The child and other cultural inventions. In F. S. Kessel & A. W. Siegel (Eds.) (pp. 26–39). New York: Praeger.

Kessen, W. (1993). A developmentalist's reflections. In G. H. Elder, Jr., J. Model, & R. D. Parke (Eds.), *Children in time and place: Developmental and historical insights* (pp. 226–229). New York: Cambridge University Press.

Kincheloe, J. L. (1991). *Teachers as researchers: Qualitative inquiry as a path to empowerment.* New York: Falmer Press.

King, N. (1987). Elementary school play: Theory and research. In J. H. Block & J. R. King (Eds.), *School play* (pp. 143–166). New York: Garland.

King, N. (1992). The impact of context on the play of young children. In S. Kessler & B. B. Swadener (Eds.), *Reconceptualizing the early childhood curriculum: Beginning the dialogue.* New York: Teachers College Press.

Kohn, A. (1999). *The schools our children deserve: Moving beyond traditional classrooms and tougher standards.* Boston: Houghton Mifflin.

Kohn, A. (2000). *The case against standardized testing: Raising the scores, ruining the schools.* Portsmouth, NH: Heinemann.

Kornhaber, M. L., & Orfield, G. (2001). High stakes testing policies: Examining their assumptions and consequences. In G. Orfield & M. L. Kornhaber (Eds.), *Raising standards or raising barriers: Inequality and high stakes testing in public education* (pp. 1–18). New York: Century Foundation Press.

Kozol, J. (1991). *Savage inequalities: Children in America's schools.* New York: Harper Perennial.

Lancy, D. F. (1984). Play in anthropological perspective. In P. K. Smith (Ed.), *Play in animals and humans.* Oxford, UK: Basil Blackwell.

Lather, P. (1984). Critical theory, curricular transformation and feminist mainstreaming. *Journal of Education, 166,* 49–62.

Lather, P. (2000). Reading the image of Rigoberta Menchú: Undecidability and langauge lessons. *International Journal of Qualitative Studies in Education, 13*(2), 153–162.

Lavine, T. (1984). *From Socrates to Sartre: The philosophic quest.* New York: Bantam Books.

Leacock, E. B. L. (1981). *Myths of male dominance: Collected articles.* New York: Monthly Review Press.

Lee, G. (2002). Young gifted girls and boys: Perspectives through the lens of gender. *Contemporary Issues in Early Childhood, 3*(3), 383–399.

Lenin, V. I. (1965 [1917]). *Imperialism, the highest stage of capitalism: A popular outline.* Peking: Foreign Languages Press.

Lerner, G. (1986). *The creation of patriarchy.* New York: Oxford University Press.

Lerner, G. (1993). *The creation of feminist consciousness: From the middle ages to eighteen-seventy.* New York: Oxford University Press.

Levin, G. (2001). High stakes testing and economic productivity. In G. Orfield & M. L. Kornhaber (Eds.), *Raising standards or raising barriers: Inequality and high stakes testing in public education* (pp. 39–50). New York: Century Foundation Press.

Lichtman, R. (1987). The illusion of maturation in an age of decline. In J. M. Broughton (Ed.), *Critical theories of psychological development* (pp. 127–148). New York: Plenum.

Lincoln, Y. S., & Cannella, G. S. (2002, April). *Qualitative research and the radical right: Cats and dogs and other natural enemies.* Paper presented at the American Educational Research Association, New Orleans, LA.

Liston, P., & Zeichner, K. (1987, April). *Critical pedagogy and teacher education.* Paper presented at the American Educational Research Association, New Orleans, LA.

Loomba, A. (1998). *Colonialism/postcolonialism.* London, UK: Routledge.

Lorde, A. (1997). Age, race, class, and sex: Women redefining difference. In A. McClintock & A. Mufti & E. Shohat (Eds.), *Dangerous liasons: Gender, nation, and postcolonial perspectives* (pp. 374–380). Minneapolis: University of Minnesota Press.

Lowe, D. (1982). *History of bourgeois perception.* Chicago: University of Chicago Press.

Luke, A., & Freebody, P. (1997). The social practices of reading. In S. Muspratt, A. Luke, P. Freebody (Eds.), *Constructing critical literacies* (pp. 185–227). Creskill, NJ: Hampton.

Luke, C. (1996). Childhood and parenting in children's popular culture and childcare magazines. In C. Luke (Ed.), *Feminisms and pedagogies of everyday life* (pp. 167–187). Albany: State University of New York Press.

Macpherson, C. B. (1962). *The political theory of possessive individualism.* Oxford, UK: Clarendon Press.

Madaus, G., & Clarke, M. (2001). The adverse impact of high stakes testing on minority students: Evidence from one hundred years of test data. In G. Orfield & M. L. Kornhaber (Eds.), *Raising standards or raising barriers: Inequality and high stakes testing in public education* (pp. 85–106). New York: Century Foundation Press.

Magdoff, H. (1978). *Imperialism: From the colonial age to the present.* New York: Monthly Review Press.

Marsh, M. M. (2001). *The social fashioning of teacher identities.* New York: Peter Land.

Marshall, W. (2001, February). Welfare reform: A progress report. *Democratic Leadership Online Community.* Retrieved March 21, 2001 from http://www.ndol.org.

Martin, B. (1997). Mathematics and social interests. In A. B. Powell & M. Frankenstein (Eds.), *Ethnomathematics: Challenging eurocentrism in mathematics education* (pp. 155–173). Albany: State University of New York Press.

Martin, J. M. (1992). *Schoolhome: Rethinking schools for changing families.* Cambridge, MA: Harvard University Press.

Mayberry, M., & Rose, E. (1999). *Meeting the challenge: Innovative feminist pedagogies in action.* New York: Routledge.

Mazrui, A. A. (1996). Progress: Illegitimate child of Judeo-Christian universalism and western ethnocentrism—A third world critique. In L. Marx & B. Mazlish (Eds.), *Progress: Fact or illusion?* (pp. 153–174). Ann Arbor: University of Michigan Press.

Mbembe, A. (2001). *On the postcolony.* Berkeley: University of California Press.

McClintock, A. (1997). No longer in future heaven: Gender, race and nationalism. In A. McClintock, A. Mufti, & E. Shohat (Eds.), *Dangerous liasons: Gender, nation and postcolonial perspectives* (pp. 89–112). Minneapolis: University of Minnesota Press.

McGillivray, A. (1997). Therapies of freedom: The colonization of aboriginal childhood. In A. Mcgillivray (Ed.), *Governing childhood* (pp. 135–199). Aldershot: Dartmouth.

McLaren, P., & Giroux, H. (1997). *Revolutionary multiculturalism.* Boulder, CO: Westview Press.

McLaren, P., & Pinkney-Pastrana, J. (2000). The search for the complicit native: Epistemic violence, historical amnesia, and the anthropologist as ideologue of empire. *International Journal of Qualitative Studies in Education, 13*(2), 163–184.

McNeil, L. (2000). *Contradictions of school reform: Educational costs of standardized testing.* New York: Routledge.

McNeil, L., & Velenzuela, A. (2001). *The harmful impact of the TAAS system of testing Texas: Beneath the accountability rhetoric.* New York: Century Foundation Press.

McWilliams, E. (1995). *In Broken images: Feminist tales for a different teacher education.* New York and London: Teachers College Press.

Mehmet, O. (1995). *Westernizing the third world: The eurocentricity of european economic development theories.* London: Routledge.

Meier, D. (2000). Educating a democracy. In J. Cohen & J. Rogers (Eds.), *Will standards save public education* (pp. 3–34). Boston: Beacon Press.

Memmi, A. (1967). *The colonizer and the colonized.* Boston: Beacon Press.

Menchú, R., & Burgos-Debray, E. (1984). *I, Rigoberta Menchú: An Indian woman in Guatemala* (A. Wright, Trans.). London: Verso.

Metcalf, S. (2002, January 28). Reading between the lines. *The Nation,* 18. Retrieved November 23, 2003 from http://www.thenation.com/doc.mhtml?i=20020128+s=metcalf

Milburn, T. (2001). Enacting "Puerto Rican time" in the United States. In M. J. Collier (Ed.), *Constituting cultural difference through discourse.* Thousand Oaks, CA: Sage.

Miller, J. (1992). Teachers, autobiography, and curriculum: Critical and feminist perspectives. In S. Kessler & B. B. Swadener (Eds.), *Reconceptualizing the early childhood curriculum: Beginning the dialogue* (pp. 102–122). New York: Teachers College Press.

Moghaddam, R. M. (1987). Psychology in the three worlds. *American Psychologist, 42*(10), 912–920.

Mohanram, R. (1999). *Black body: Women, colonialism, and space.* Minneapolis: University of Minnesota Press.

Mohanty, C. T. (1991). Under western eyes: Feminist scholarship and colonial discourses. In C. T. Mohanty, & A. Russo, & L. Torres (Eds.), *Third world women and the politics of feminism* (pp. 255–277). Bloomington: Indiana University Press.

Morss, J. R. (1990). *The biologising of childhood: Developmental psychology and the Darwinian myth.* London, UK: Lawrence Erlbaum.

Munck, R., & O'Hearn, D. (Eds.). (1999). *Critical development theory: Contributions to a new paradigm.* London: Zed Books.

Nakata, J. (1995). Modern Malay women and the message of the veil. In W. J. Karim (Ed.), *Male and female in developing Southeast Asia.* Washington, DC: Berg Publishers.

Nandy, A. (1993). *The intimate enemy.* Delhi, India: Oxford University Press.

Neihardt, J. G. (1961). *Black elk speaks.* Lincoln: University of Nebraska Press.

Ngugi, W. T. (1981). *Decolonizing the mind.* London: James Currey.

Ngugi, W. T. (1993). *Moving the centre: The struggle for cultural freedoms.* London: James Currey.

Nicholas, D. (1991). Childhood in medieval Europe. In J. M. Hawes & N. R. Hiner (Eds.), *Children in historical and comparative perspective.* Westport, CT: Greenwood Press.

Nkrumah, K. (1965). *Neocolonialism: The last state of imperialism.* London: Heinemann.

Noddings, N. (1992). *The challenge to care in schools: An alternative approach to education.* New York and London: Teachers College Press.

Nsamenang, A. B. (1992). *Human development in cultural context: A third world perspective.* Newbury Park, CA: Sage.

Ohanian, S. (2002). *What happened to recess and why are our children struggling in kindergarten?* New York: McGraw Hill.

Olssen, M. (1999). *Michel Foucault: Materialism and education.* Westport, CT: Bergin & Garvey.

Onuma, Y. (1999). Toward an intercivilizational approach to human rights. In J. Bauer & D. Bell (Eds.), *The east Asian challenge for human rights.* Cambridge, MA: Cambridge University Press.

Overtrup, J. (1997). A voice for children in statistical and social accounting: A plea for children's right to be heard. In A. James & A. Prout (Eds.), *Constructing and reconstructing childhood: Contemporary issues in the sociological study of childhood* (pp. 85–103). Washington, DC: Falmer.

Paechter, C. (1998). *Educating the other: Gender, power and schooling.* London: Falmer.

Pagano, J. (1990). *Exiles and communities: Teaching in the patriarchal wilderness.* Albany: State University of New York Press.

Paley, V. (1997). *The girl with the brown crayon.* Cambridge, MA: Harvard University Press.

Palsson, G. (1999). Human-environmental relations: Orientalism, paternalism and communalism. In P. Descola & G. Palsson (Eds.), *Nature and society: Anthropological perspectives* (Vols. pp. 63–81). New York: Routledge.

Papastergiadis, N. (2000). *The turbulence of migration: Globalization, deterritorialization and hybridity.* Malden, MA: Polity Press.

Parry, B. (1987). Problems in current theories of colonial discourse. *Oxford Literary Review, 9,* 27–58.

Pers, P., & Salemink, O. (1999). Introduction: Locating the colonial subjects of anthropology. In P. Pers & O. Salemink (Eds.), *Colonial subjects: Essays on the practical history of anthropology* (pp. 1–52). Ann Arbor: University of Michigan Press.

Popkewitz, T., & Brennan, M. (1999). Restructuring of social and political theory in education: Foucault and a social epistemology of school practices. In T. Popkewitz & M. Brennan (Eds.), *Foucault's challenge: Discourse, knowledge, and power in education* (pp. 3–38). New York: Teachers College Press.

Porter, E. (1996). Women and friendships: Pedagogies of care and relationality. In C. Luke (Ed.), *Feminisms and pedagogies of everyday life* (pp. 56–79). Albany: State University of New York Press.

Potiki, R. (1991). Confirming identity and telling the stories: A woman's perspective on Maori theater. In R. D. Plessis (Ed.), *Feminist voices: Women studies tests for Aoteroa/New Zealand.* Auckland: Oxford University Press.

Powell, A. B., & Frankenstein, M. (1997). Introduction. In A. B. Power & M. Frankenstein (Eds.), *Ethnomathematics: challenging eurocentrism in mathematics education* (pp. 1–5). Albany: State University of New York Press.

Pratt, M. L. (2001). I, Rigoberta Menchú and the "culture wars." In A. Arias (Ed.), *The Rigoberta Menchú Controversy* (pp. 29–57). Minneapolis: University of Minnesota Press.

Puntambekar, S. V. (1973). The Hindu concept of human rights. In UNESCO (Ed.), *Human rights: Comments and interpretations.* Westport, CT: Greenwood Press.

Rajchman, J. (1984). The story of Foucault's history. *Social Text, 8.*

Rector, R. (2000). *Reviewing the revolution: Conservative successes in the 104th congress.* Heritage Foundation. Retrieved March, 2001 from http://www.heritage.org/heritage/congress/chap.5.html

Rensenbrink, C. W. (2001). *All in our places: Feminist challenges in elementary school classrooms.* Lanham, MD: Rowman & Littlefield.

Riley, D. (1983). *War in the nursery: Theories of child and mother.* London, UK: Virago.

Rivers, W.H.R. (1913) Report on anthropological research outside America. In W.H.R. Rivers, A. E. Jenks & S. G. Morley (eds.). *Reports upon the present condition and future needs of the science of anthropology* (pp. 5–28). Washington, D.C.: Carnegie Institute.

Rockhill, K. (1993). Gender, language and the politics of literacy. In B. V. Street (Ed.), *Cross-cultural approaches to literacy* (pp. 156–175). Cambridge: Cambridge University Press.

Rodney, W. (1989). *How Europe underdeveloped Africa.* Nairobi: Heinemann Kenya.

Rose, N. (1985). *The psychological complex: Psychology, politics and society in England 1869–1939.* London, UK: Routledge & Kegan Paul.

Rose, N. (1990). *Governing the soul: The shaping of the private self.* London, UK: Routledge.

Rosser, S. (1990). *Female friendly science.* New York: Pergamon Press.

Rossiter, M. W. (1982). *Women scientists in America: Struggles and strategies to 1940*. Baltimore: Johns Hopkins University Press.

Rostow, W. W. (1960). *The stages of economic growth: A non-comunist manifesto*. Cambridge: Cambridge University Press.

Rouse, J. (1996). Power/knowledge. In G. Gutting (Ed.), *The Cambridge companion to Foucault* (pp. 92–114). Cambridge: Cambridge University Press.

Rousseau, J. J. (1933). *Emile*. New York: E. P. Dutton.

Russell, M. S. (1985). Black eyed blues connections: Teaching black women. In M. Culley & C. Portuges (Eds.), *Gendered subjects: The dynamics of feminist teaching*. New York: Routledge & Kegan Paul.

Sacks, P. (1999). *Standardized minds: The high price of America's testing culture and what we can do to change it*. Cambridge, MA: Perseus Books.

Said, E. (1978). *Orientalism*. London: Routledge and Kegan Paul.

Said, E. (1984). *The world, the text and the critic*. London: Faber & Faber.

Said, E. (1993). *Culture and imperialism*. London: Chatto & Windus.

Said, E. (1995). Secular interpretation, the geographical element and the methodology of imperialism. In G. Prakash (Ed.), *After colonialism* (pp. 21–40). Princeton, NJ: Princeton University Press.

Said, E. (1996). Orientalism. In P. Mongia (Ed.), *Contemporary postcolonial theory: A reader* (pp. 205–225). London: Arnold.

Sandoval, C. (2000). *Methodology of the oppressed: Theory out of bounds*. Minneapolis: University of Minnesota Press.

Sawicki, J. (1991). *Disciplining Foucault: Feminism, power, and the body*. New York: Routledge.

Schiebinger, L. (1989). *The mind has no sex: Women in the origins of modern science*. Cambridge, MA: Harvard University Press.

Scott, D. (1995). Colonial governmentality. *Social Text, 43*, 191–200.

Scott, J. C. (1998). *Seeing like a state: How certain schemes to improve the human condition have failed*. New Haven, CT: Yale University Press.

Seed, P. (1991). Failing to marval: Atahaulpa's encounter with the word. *Latin American Research Review, 26*, 7–32.

Seiter, E. (1991). Toys are us: Marketing to children and parents. *Cultural Studies, 6*, 232–247.

Seth, V. (1981). *Mappings*. New Delhi: Penguin/Viking Books.

Shakeshaft, C. (1989). *Women in educational administration*. Newbury Park, CA: Sage.

Sharpe, J. (1993). *Allegories of empire: The figure of woman in the colonial text*. Minneapolis: University of Minnesota Press.

Shiva, V. (1989). *Staying alive: Women, ecology and development*. London: Zed Books.

Shklovsky, V. (1965 [1917]). Art as technique (L. T. Lemon & M. J. Reis, Trans.). In L. T. Lemon & M. J. Reis (Eds.), *Russian formalist criticism* (pp. 3–24). Lincoln: University of Nebraska Press.

Shohat, E. (1992). Notes on the "post-colonial." *Social Text, 31/32*, 99–113.

Silin, J. G. (1995). *Sex, death, and the education of children: Our passion for ignorance in the age of AIDS*. New York: Teachers College Press.

Singer, E. (1992). *Child care and the psychology of development*. New York: Routledge.

Skultans, V. (1977). Bodily madness and the blush. In J. Blacking (Ed.), *The anthropology of the body*. London: Academic Press.

Sleman, S. (1994). The scramble for post-colonialism. In C. Tiffin & A. Lawson (Eds.), *Describing empire: Postcolonialism and textuality* (pp. 15–32). London: Routledge.

Smith, L. T. (1999). *Decolonizing methodologies: Research and indigenous peoples*. London, UK: Zed Books.

Smith, P. K. (1980). Shared care for young children: alternative models to monotropism. *Merrill Palmer Quarterly, 6*, 371–389.

Sommers, C. H. (1994). *Who stole feminism? How women have betrayed women.* New York: Simon & Schuster.

Spelman, E. (1988). *Inessential woman: Problems of exclusion in feminist thought.* Boston: Beacon Press.

Spivak, G. C. (1988). Can the subaltern speak? In C. Nelson & L. Grossberg (Eds.), *Marxism and the interpretation of culture.* Urbana: University of Illinois Press.

Spivak, G. C. (1996). Poststructuralism, marginality, postcoloniality, and value. In P. Mongia (Ed.), *Contemporary postcolonial theory: A reader* (pp. 198–223). London: Arnold.

Spivak, G. C. (1999). *A critique of postcolonial reason: Toward a history of the vanishing present.* Cambridge, MA: Harvard University Press.

Spring, J. (2001). *Globalization and educational rights: An intercivilizational analysis.* Mahwah, NJ: Lawrence Erlbaum.

Squier, S. (1996). Fetal subjects and maternal objects: Reproductive technologies and the new maternal/fetal relation. *Journal of Medicine and Philosophy, 21*(5), 517.

Stepan, N. L. (1982). *The idea of race in science.* Hamden, CO: Archon Books.

Stephan (2001) is Gonzalez-Stephan, B. (2001). The teaching machine for the wild citizen. In I. Rodriguex (ed.). *Latin American subaltern studies reader* (pp. 313–340). Durham, NC: Duke University Press.

Stocking, G. (1991), *Colonial situations: Essays on the contextualization of ethnographic knowledge.* Madison: University of Wisconsin Press.

Stocking, G. W. (2001). *Delimiting anthropology: Occasional essays and reflections.* Madison: University of Wisconsin Press.

Stoler, A. L. (1992, February 7). *Sexual affronts and racial frontiers: European identities and the cultural politics of exclusion in colonial Southeast Asia.* Paper presented at the Davis Center Seminar, Princeton University, Princeton, NJ.

Stoler, A. L. (1995). *Race and the education of desire: Foucault's history of sexuality and the colonial order of things.* Durham, NC: Duke University Press.

Stoler, A. L. (1997). Making empire respectable: The politics of race and sexual morality in twentieth century colonial cultures. In A. McClintock, A. Mufti, & E. Shohat (Eds.), *Dangerous liasions: Gender, nation and postcolonial perspectives* (pp. 344–373). Minneapolis: University of Minnesota Press.

Stoler, A. L., & Cooper, F. (1997). Between metropole and colony: Rethinking a research aganda. In F. Cooper & A. L. Stoler (Eds.), *Tensions of empire: Colonial cultures in a bourgeois world* (pp. 1–58). Berkeley: University of California Press.

Stoll, D. (1999). *Rigoberta Menchú and the story of all poor Guatemalans.* Boulder, CO: Westview Press.

Stuckey, J. E. (1991). *The violence of literacy.* Portsmouth, NH: Heinemann.

Sullivan, E. (1974). A study of Kohlberg's structural theory of moral development: A critique of liberal social science ideology. *Human Development, 20,* 352–375.

Swann, J., & Graddol, D. (1994). Gender equalities in classroom talk. In D. Graddol & J. Maybin & B. Stierer (Eds.), *Researching language and literacy in social context.* Clevedon: Multilingual Matters.

Szebo, L. & Cebotarev, E.A. (1990). Women's work patterns: A time allocation study of rural families in St. Lucia. *Canadian Journal of Development Studies,* 11 (2), 259–78.

Taylor-Allen, A. (1982). Spiritual motherhood: German feminists and the kindergarten movement, 1848–1911. *History of Education Quarterly, 22,* 319–339.

Thobani, S. (1992). Making the links: South Asian women and the struggle for reproductive rights. *Canadian Women's Studies/Cahiers de la femme, 13*(1), 19–22.

Thompson, E. P. (1963). *The Making of the English Working Class.* New York: Pantheon.

Tiffin, C., & Lawson, A. (1994). *De-Scribing empire, postcolonialism and textuality.* London, UK: Routledge.

Tobin, J., & Davidson, D. (1990). The ethics of polyvocal ethnography: Empowering vrs. textualizing children and teachers. *International Journal of Qualitative Studies in Education, 3*, 271–284.

Tobin, J. J. (1997). Playing doctor in two cultures: The United States and Ireland. In H. Kozicki (Ed.). New Haven, CT: Yale University Press.

Tong, R. (1989). *Feminist thought: A comprehensive introduction.* Boulder, CO: Westview Press.

Tong, R. (2001). Is a global bioethics possible as well as desirable? A millennial feminist response. In R. Tong (Ed.), *Globalizing feminist bioethics: Cross cultural perspectives* (pp. 27–37). Boulder, CO: Westview Press.

Trattner, W. I. (1999). *From poor law to welfare state: A history of social welfare in America.* New York: Free Press.

Tucker, V. (1999). The myth of development: A critique of Eurocentric discourse. In R. Munck & D. O'Hearn (Eds.), *Critical development theory: Contributions to a new paradigm* (pp. 1–26). London: Zed Books.

Urton, G. (1981). *At the crossroads of earth and sky: An Andian cosmology.* Austin: University of Texas Press.

Vaughan, M. (1991). *Curing their ills: Colonial power and African illness.* Stanford, CA: Stanford University Press.

Vaughan, M. (1993). Madness and colonialism, colonialism as madness. *Pajdauma, 39,* 45–55.

Viruru, R. (2001). *Early childhood education: Postcolonial perspectives from India.* New Delhi: Sage.

Viruru, R., & Cannella, G. S. (1999, October). *A postcolonial scrutiny of early childhood education.* Paper presented at the JCT Conference, Dayton, OH.

Viruru, R., & Cannella, G. S. (2001a). Early childhood education and postcolonial possibilities. In R. Viruru (Ed.), *Decolonizing early childhood education: An Indian perspective* (pp. 137–156). New Delhi: Sage.

Viruru, R., & Cannella, G. S. (2001b). Postcolonial ethnography, young children, and voice. In S. Grieshaber & G. S. Cannella (Eds.), *Embracing identities in early childhood education: Diversity and possibilities* (pp. 158–172). New York: Teachers College Press.

Voneche, J. J. (1987). The difficulty of being a child in French-speaking countries. In J. M. Broughton (Ed.), *Critical theories of psychological development* (pp. 61–86). New York: Plenum Press.

Walcott, D. (1995). The muse of history. In B. Ashcroft, G. Griffiths, & H. Tiffin (Eds.), *The postcolonial studies reader* (pp. 370–374). New York: Routledge.

Walkerdine, V. (1984). Developmental psychology and the child-centred pedagogy: The insertion of Piaget into early education. In J. Henriques, W. Holloway, C. Urwin, C. Venn, & V. Walkerdine (Eds.), *Changing the subject: Psychology, social regulation and subjectivity* (pp. 153–202). London: Methuen.

Walkerdine, V. (1988). *The mastery of reason: Cognitive development and the production of rationality.* London, UK: Routledge.

Walkerdine, V. (1989). *Counting girls out.* London, UK: Virago Press.

Walkerdine, V. (1997). *Daddy's girl: Young girls and popular culture.* Cambridge, MA: Harvard University Press.

Walkerdine, V. (2000). Boys and precocious girls: Regulating childhood at the end of the millennium. *Contemporary Issues in Early Childhood, 1*(1), 3–22.

Walkerdine, V., & Lucey, H. (1989). *Democracy in the kitchen: Regulating mothers and socialising daughters.* London, UK: Virago.

Wallerstein, I. (1979). *The capitalist world economy: Essays.* Cambridge: Cambridge University Press.

Wallerstein, I. (1983). *Historical capitalism.* London: Verso Editions.

Wallerstein, I. (1984). *The politics of the world-economy: The states, the movements, and the civilizations: Essays.* Cambridge: Cambridge University Press.

Waterman, P. (1998). *Globalization, social movements, and the new internationalisms.* London: Mansell.

Weaver, R. K. (2000). *Ending welfare as we know it.* Washington, DC: Brookings Institution Press.

Weber, E. (1984). *Ideas influencing early childhood education.* New York: Teachers College Press.

Weiner, M. (Ed.). (1966). *Modernization: The dynamics of growth.* New York: Basic Books.

Williams, M. S. (1998). *Voice, trust, and memory.* Princeton, NJ: Princeton University Press.

Woodhead, M. (1990). Psychology and the cultural construction of children's needs. In A. James & A. Prout (Eds.), *Constructing and reconstructing childhood* (pp. 60–78). New York: Falmer.

Woollett, A., & Phoenix, A. (1996). Motherhood as pedagogy: Developmental psychology and the accounts of mothers of young children. In C. Luke (Ed.), *Feminisms and pedagogies of everyday life* (pp. 80–102). Albany: State University of New York Press.

World Commission on Environment & Development. (1987). *Our common future.* New York: Oxford University Press.

Wyer, M. (2001). Over the edge: Developing feminist frameworks in the sciences and women's studies. In M. Mayberry, & B. Subramaniam, & L. H. Weasel (Eds.), *Feminist science studies: A new generation* (pp. 72–81). New York: Routledge.

Young, R. J. C. (2001). *Postcolonialism: An historical introduction.* Oxford, UK: Blackwell Publishers.

INDEX

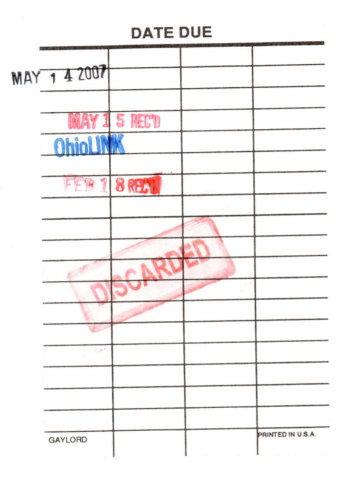